NAPTIME

AT THE O.K. CORRAL

NAPTIME AT THE O.K.CORRAL

SHANE'S Beginner's Guide to Childhood Ethnography

BY SALLY CAMPBELL GALMAN

Routledge
Taylor & Francis Group

NEW YORK AND LONDON

First published 2019
by Routledge
711 Third Avenue, New York, NY 10017

and by Routledge
2 Park Square, Milton Park, Abingdon, Oxon, OX14 4RN

Routledge is an imprint of the Taylor & Francis Group, an informa business

Library of Congress Control Number: 2017952409

ISBN: 978-1-138-57225-6 (hbk)
ISBN: 978-1-61132-845-5 (pbk)
ISBN: 978-0-203-71247-4 (ebk)

Table of Contents

Sally Campbell Galman
is a Professor of Child
and Family Studies at the
University of Massachusetts,
Amherst. She lives on
a dirt road in rural
Western Massachusetts
with her daughters,
husband, and many cats.

www.sallycampbellgalman.com

Chapter One

NO COUNTRY FOR OLD (OR EVEN MIDDLE AGED, OR ADOLESCENT) MEN

Why Studying Children is Different

What do you MEAN "Do I have the right qualifications?" I used to babysit for her! Let's see...

candidate must ha
◎ ethnographic meth
◎ qualitative data analysis methodo
◎ background in childhood studies or chil
◎ advanced skills in

childhood shmildhood! I've got it in the BAG!

...besides- I've been a child, right? Small people means smaller methods! Put some unicorn stickers on the consent forms and hand out candy at the interview and it's great!

But SHANE. Dr. Parous is going to want to see SOME kind of background in childhood. What do you even know about child development or about the anthropology of childhood or anything?!?

Development? Sheesh. Kids get BIGGER as they get OLDER. I'm applying.

Let me know if you want me to proofread anything...

LATER THAT NIGHT

I'll show HIM. I'm going to get that post-doc. I KNOW I can...

Studying children in this way is to illuminate and to generously construct them. NOT to further marginalize them.

MOST importantly, children are NOT containers for future economic productivity.

FUTURE WORKER

FUTURE WORKER

FUTURE WORKER

Future Worker

Hmm... Let's test these children to see how much math they know. Yes! They must be prepared to work in STEM fields.

Much educational research and conversation is guilty of framing children in this way.

But this is not our project!

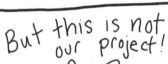

I AM A PERSON NOW!

I have value NOW As what I am NOW.

Ⓛ

Teacher, why must we walk in a line?

Because you must learn to follow rules so you can be a good worker, Shane.

Hmmm.

I guess I never thought of it like that before.

GREAT! Now let's move on to the second Ⓡ ...

Right NOW!

RiGHT NOW!

Imagine that people only cared about what would be happening in the future...

SHE COULD GROW UP TO BE A DOCTOR QUICK LET'S ALL TEST HER APTITUDE IN MATH SCIENCE AND ENROLL HE IN SUMMER MATH PR

mommy, my dolly lost an eye.

I just wanted my doll fixed.

sigh.

This is related to our last **R** about children being real people NOW but this also speaks to the research we do.

We want the ethnography of childhood to focus on being descriptive, not predictive.

The anthropology of childhood is part of the universe of cultural anthropology. So, that is NOT educational research like testing.

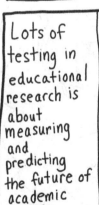

Lots of testing in educational research is about measuring and predicting the future of academic stuff.

Instead, we are about describing and seeking to UNDERSTAND children and childhoods RIGHT NOW.

You fixed my doll

We believe the RIGHT NOW has lots of value and mystery and wonder, best explored in naturalistic settings by descriptive research.

NOW - wait RIGHT there you literal kid you - you are WRONG.

Really?

It says right here in my big book that anthropologists of all kinds study children

GIANT ANTHRO TEXT

Not just cultural anthropologists, either.

GIANT

Our <u>methods</u> as ethnographers also help us with this ✶Rethinking✶

While lots of research with children takes place in laboratory settings...

Or, even in the case of naturalistic studies, draws exclusively from interviews...

tell me about being a baby.

No comment

Ethnographers rely primarily on PARTICIPANT OBSERVATION — and that helps position the researcher as LEARNER.

interesting...

I AM A PIRATE!

You know, you are RIGHT! I feel like spending all that TIME watching and *learning* is an ongoing reminder to Rethink!

AHOY MATEY!

Yes! By Rethinking your stance and positioning yourself as a learner, your research will be that much better.

can I be a pirate, too?

NO.

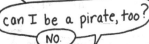

James, Jenks & Prout (1998) said it best:

"Children's culture and childhood [are] an independent place with its own folklore, rituals, rules and normative constraints... within a system that is unfamiliar to [adults] and therefore to be revealed through research" (p. 29).

They agree that children's lives and worlds deserve "detailed annotation" that is meaningful and not just cute stories or nostalgic projects.

But what is a 🐻 NOSTALGIA PROJECT?

Think of it as a cute story that reduces children to just a cute anecdote that appeals to adults.

James, Jenks & Prout (1998) call this "generating whimsical tales" (p.30) instead of offering a MEANINGFUL account of childlife.

I'm a PERSON, Not a cute toy.

Well... it is really fun to tell cute stories. I love to watch kids doing cute things!

... but I hear what you are saying.

Sigh.

OK, NOW I'm READY! I'll find some kids, observe and describe. EASY PEASY!

Not so fast! Where exactly do you expect to FIND children?

and of course study design... but that will come later.

Uh... School?

good start – but not necessarily. Lots of people, especially in Western contexts, think children are best found in institutional settings, like schools.

But that isn't always the case and the assumption reflects unexamined biases...

not all learning happens in "schools"

my children keep me company at work, and while they help out, I teach them!

There are lots of places all over the world where children are not always in schools or childcare, segregated from adults.

*this is not desirable, but child labor is alive and well — in countries all over the world. It is closer to you than you think. ☹

AND, I can probably learn a lot about people and culture by where I find children!

Yep!

But I am still confused about one thing... Children participate in culture — resisting it, acquiring it, producing it, etc. But is there such a thing as CHILDREN'S CULTURE?

NOW you're talking! There are LOADS of layers to that question. Let's *jump in!*

The easy answer is YES. Children have cultures that are theirs, " an independent place with its own folklore, rituals, rules, and normative constraints." (as James, Jenks and Prout tell us)

But it is also NOT that simple. For example,

SING ALONG WITH US! ♪ Bunny ... Bunny

Children's POPULAR CULTURE isn't something they produce, but they *do* negotiate and engage and retell and rewrite and PLAY WITH IT.

If you really want to be an *ethnographer of childhood* you should familiarize yourself with the popular culture landscapes that are part of your participants' contexts.

This could mean watching the TV shows they watch, and finding out what toys and games are popular

And remember your STANCE → bracket your adult ideas and try to LEARN.

It might seem like a LOT of popular culture input but it is important — and it is also key to *remember* that children are agentive consumers in relationship and negotiation with *culture*

Mitchell & Reid-Walsh (2002) lay out some VERY useful foundations for thinking about *children and popular culture*

"Popular culture, especially mass-media culture, is often constructed as a monolithic giant, while the child is depicted as a powerless object who is about to be consumed. The researchers see themselves as off-screen saviors, rushing in to save the child who is unable to save himself or herself. The researchers, battling and conquering evil, play the role of the prince in fairy tales." (p. 2)

So, hang onto your hat and keep the "Three R's" in mind.

... But don't miss out, either. Popular culture is a good entry point to understand *childhood*.

DRAGONS AND PRINCESSES

But just watching loads and loads of kids' TV seems, uh, too easy?

Nobody said anything about easy!

As we've said, studying children is DIFFERENT. You aren't a child NOW— and your *memories* of being a child are NOT adequate, and you are an ADULT with adult ideas.

Kids' TV is AWFUL!

It's possible that some children's culture makes adults *uncomfortable*

That may be...

But here's another thing— what is the difference between children's culture and "Kinderculture"?

GIANT BOOK

is it the same, or different?

it is—and it isn't...

great.

Kinderculture

a "corporate construction of childhood."

(steinberg & kincheloe, 1997)

at its most basic, it is "culture" that is marketed TO children, and constructed by corporations to create consumers.

You NEED MORE STUFF

Media and marketing pervade much of children's cultures, but Kinderculture is not the same thing.

$19.99 YOU NEED this thing!

BUY!

$tuff!

A children's culture is all of the rules, norms, practices and things children make, do and use, as well as things made for them or sometimes even about them or around them.

Think about the things some cultures make FOR children, specifically.

ADULT SPOON

BABY SPOON

there are many examples.

But KINDERCULTURE seeks to construct the child as *consumer*.

"using fantasy and desire, corporate functionaries... let children know that the most exciting things life can provide are produced by your friends in corporate America... The economics lesson is powerful when it is repeated hundreds of thousands of times." (steinberg & kincheloe, 1997)

I feel sick.

Don't. Children know a lot about culture.

They manipulate it, twist and turn it, resist it, incorporate and even dismantle it! They are pretty savvy.

TA·DA!

As a researcher, you can think in complex ways, and watch to learn how children stake out *cultures*.

And it demonstrates how this work is *different!*

A really fascinating place to see all this come together is in James' (1989) work on the "*ket* aesthetic". James describes how children take ownership of and make use of what adults would call garbage, unappetizing food, or trash.

EXPLODING CANDY BOMB!

CHOC-O-CHOC-O-CHOCO...

In James' study, British children adopted the term "ket"— which basically means "rubbish"— to describe the candies purchased with their pocket money.

WAX LIPS
POP CANDY

They are JUST the sort of thing adults can't STAND.

ugh.
yum!

Right! When I would babysit, the kids would delight in eating the NASTIEST most SUGARY, HORRIBLE stuff they could find. It made me GAG!

CRISPY CHOC-O FOOD DYE

SO SO HOT CAUSTIC HOTS!

But what this *Really* was, writes James, is:

"children's appropriation and transformation of the term [ket] as a metaphor for the relationship between the world of children and adults, one in which children construct and reinterpret adult practices." (404)

Methodologically speaking, it's hard to keep one's _stance_ intact.

Mitchell & Reid-Walsh (2002) remind us that lots of children's popular culture is not comfy viewing for adults.

From an adult's position—a classed, raced, gendered position, children's popular culture may not be what they consider "quality" play.

Please please pleeeeeeeease buy me a FART BEAR!

At one researcher's* field site, parents were happiest when children were provided with constructive playthings—wooden blocks, clay, paints and cloth dolls, etc.

These same parents became upset when children had access to popular culture—like fashion dolls, licensed characters and movie merchandise. (even though children loved it)

This becomes further complicated when your research site is a school, where many classrooms forbid or otherwise censor popular culture toys or play.

So, you might need to go somewhere else to really see children engage with popular culture.

or look for it in the margins and liminal spaces.

* see Galman 2017 ☺

It's ALSO about shoring up the BOUNDARIES between worlds...

adult world / KID WORLD

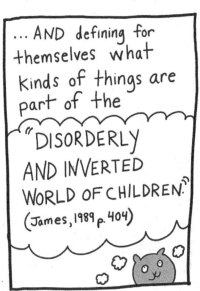

...AND defining for themselves what kinds of things are part of the "DISORDERLY AND INVERTED WORLD OF CHILDREN." (James, 1989 p.404)

Like in LORD of the FLIES?!?

no. not really.

Think of it like this:

Adult culture can be future-oriented, rule-driven and somber.

I am an accountant.

I follow rules and I sit nicely at the lunch table.

The "ket aesthetic" is really about asserting a bit of agency and control

Instead of sitting nicely at table we're eating gummy worms off the pavement!

I'm rotting my teeth!

For people who spend most of the time under adult control, they have elaborate cultures and aesthetics in place.

I just thought they wanted the sugar. But it's so much more than just chewed up gummy bears in the carpet!

And that's just the START. Hop in my wagon and we'll get going!

Red Wagon

HOMEWORK!

for chapter one

Will there be a TEST?!?

HOWDY! Now that you have READ *Chapter One*, you should follow-up with some REFLECTION, OBSERVATION, & JOURNALING!

1. Reflect:

THINK ABOUT THE CHILDREN'S CULTURES IN YOUR CONTEXT. WHAT KINDS OF MATERIAL ARE PRESENT? MADE BY WHOM? FOR WHOM? HOW DO YOU KNOW?

2. Observe:

OBSERVE A CHILDREN'S SETTING, LIKE A PLAYGROUND OR COMMUNITY PLAYSPACE. HOW DOES *careful* OBSERVATION OF CHILDREN FEEL DIFFERENT OR THE SAME AS OBSERVING ADULTS? WHY?

3. Journal

WHAT ARE YOUR *ideas* ABOUT CHILDREN AND CULTURE? WHERE DO YOU THINK THESE CAME FROM?

Chapter Two

LITTLE BRITCHES

What is a child?

There isn't <u>ONE</u> idyllic childhood but rather a variety of childhoods experienced by children living in different CONTEXTS.

Scholars and others have been working to get past the idea of a single, normative childhood against which other childhoods are evaluated and cast as aberrant.

Think about images of usually white, western cherubic children and how they are idealized as icons of the "gold standard" in childhood.

yeah!

And this isn't an artifact of a distant past, either. An image search of "kids" brings you mostly white suburban Western children.

meanwhile, one might see Black and Brown children from a range of contexts starving and dying in TV ads.

FOR ONLY 6 cents a day YOU CAN SAVE CHILDREN'S LIVES which must by definition be miserable.

uh... I DON'T NEED SAVING.

The message about which is a legitimate "childhood" is clear. Some media even use terms like "lost childhood" to describe the experiences of the urban, the poor, and basically ANY CHILD WHO IS NOT WHITE, WEALTHY AND WESTERN.

But <u>all</u> children's experiences are childhoods, and all are shaped by material circumstances, beliefs, practices and conditions—just like all childhoods.

There is no one normative childhood. ALL childhoods are products of larger structures, and the concept of childhood is SLIPPERY and *always* CHANGING.

Okay... so let me see if I have this right:

Children are NOT a single, homogeneous group — and they have lots of diverse experiences...

... and all of these experiences constitute _Childhoods_ — there is not one NORMATIVE set of experiences that makes up "*childhood*."

... AND, children are not just *EXPERIENCING* they are also *CONSTRUCTING* childhoods.

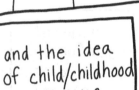

and the idea of child/childhood is DYNAMIC.

WHEEEEE!

"THERE IS NOT ONE CHILDHOOD, BUT MANY, FORMED AT THE INTERSECTION OF DIFFERENT CULTURAL SOCIAL AND ECONOMIC SYSTEMS, NATURAL AND MAN-MADE PHYSICAL ENVIRONMENTS. DIFFERENT POSITIONS IN SOCIETY PRODUCE DIFFERENT EXPERIENCES." —FRØNES, 1993 p.1

says it all!

We'll come back to more conversation about this but for now you've got a good start!

It makes sense.

I always thought about childhood in a way that was a little, well, _cute_ and _wobbly_.

BING!

elevator's here!

asofjewofjsdofjsdoifjsdoifjsdofijsdoifjsd

So, by your logic, a CHILD is defined as NOT AN ADULT.

When does being an adult BEGIN?

hmm...

18! In the U.S. it is at age 18... but you can drink at 21... and drive at 16... so...

Uh... but then a 17 year old is a child... who can drive...?

Well, no— you can get married at 15 in some places in the U.S. And my cousin had her Quinceañera at 15...

That meant she is an adult now — and people have Bar/Bat Mitzvahs at age 13 — but you are still not REALLY an adult at those ages — I think...

It is confusing because childhood is much more COMPLICATED than just how old a person is.

I'm so confused.

AND it's DYNAMIC, and there are MULTIPLE childhoods AND I'll NEVER BE ABLE TO DEFINE IT COMPLETELY...

But *why* should I? Maybe it is SUPPOSED to be FLUID — NOT rigidly defined? What difference does it make when childhood ENDS?!?

AFTER ALL, CHILDHOOD IS SOCIALLY CONSTRUCTED! HA!

Yes — BUT even if the concept is CONSTRUCTED, the child is REAL.

SO, THE BILLION DOLLAR QUESTION IS WHAT CAME FIRST?

AND WHAT IS REAL?

AND WHAT IS THE MEANING? AND WHAT CAN WE UNDERSTAND?

Everyone wonders about what childhoods are and are not, how they are defined and why.

Philippe Ariés, a French historian of child and family wrote a big, juicy, and really quite wide-open-to-criticism book in 1960 in which he claims that childhood did not really exist historically. It is, he writes, a rather new thing and invention of more contemporary times.

Philippe writes that an historical analysis shows us a world, prior to the modern era, wherein adults saw children as DISPOSABLE, their lives as necessarily brutal and short.

medieval times are no fun.

TRASH

mini adult

"In medieval society the idea of childhood did not exist." (p. 128)

Ariés didn't necessarily say childhood was always *awful*, but he did suggest that parents had less emotional attachment to their children forced to cope with frequent child deaths, making little distinction for youth.

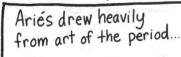

Ariés drew heavily from art of the period...

... which at the time featured children dressed as small adults...

And lots of baby Jesuses in medieval art were painted to look like little old men.

So, art might not be all that reliable as a source - and critics think Ariés took all that art too literally.

These are just my fancy portrait clothes! Not my play clothes!

Childhood __existed__ in its many forms, and there is evidence in the historical record that children were loved and cherished and afforded special status, distinct from adults.

Ancient Roman pull toy of horse and rider.

Meanwhile, Anthropologists say children have always, and in most historical contexts, been afforded special status.

English monks in the early Anglo-Saxon period wrote special books and puzzles to help children learn.

Most cultures have made sense of childhood somehow, and cared for child members.

Archaeologists in Iran found that prehistoric peoples clearly cared for disabled children, often sustaining them for life.

In many Western contexts people have tried to understand children using frames made by developmental psychologists — like Piaget.

Not Piaget! I barely passed that course!

Ye Olde GIANT BOOK of CHILD DEVELOPMENT

Don't freak out! It is just one meaning system used to make sense of children!

People love to make sense of things with patterns. Piaget was good at finding patterns.

OK- I can see how a tendency to sort and find patterns influences thinking about how children grow and learn

Little Red Schoolhouse

And that can be seen clearly in U.S. cultural practices – especially around schooling.

Now you're talking!

...And the early 20th century focus on factory models.

... and EFFICIENCY demands that we use our understanding of childhood as a pattern to GROUP and SORT and thereby maximize said "EFFICIENCY"...

... even though people in nature are not sorted this way.

So, conception builds function: Our way of creating structures for children, like schools, would probably be different if we didn't build our understanding of children on developmental psychology, with its emphasis on sorting.

If, as Ariés described, we were medieval Europeans who did not separate children from adults, seeing them as small adults, we wouldn't shape many of our institutions and practices the way we currently do.

In the U.S. and many other places, we even use these patterns to chop childhood into defined sections.

Infancy

early childhood

middle childhood

terrifying adolesence

You can see how these chunks fit nicely with western schooling...

...convenient?

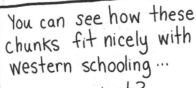
2.9 → 5 years old = preschool

AGE 4

even though not all 4 year olds are in the same developmental place.

I totally wasn't going to go there but are we saying that STAGES —

- developmental theory - isn't LEGIT?

Whoa!

MIND = BLOWN

NO! NO NO NO NO NO! We're saying it's ONE totally "legit" way of thinking - but not the only one.

Whew - it's really not a good feeling to blow your own mind.

Well, you ARE onto something. Let's keep thinking...

Anthropologists of childhood think that the stages of development in "ages & stages" theories are patterns that can be true for most children most of the time — but not ALL children ALL of the time.

Then there are the theorists and researchers who want to chuck the whole thing and get on with something less normative.

DOWN WITH PIAGET!
NO MORE AGES AND STAGES!

But really most of the time development is seen as happening in CONTEXT, and most folks agree that CULTURE can also drive development

NOW I'M REALLY LOST.

OKAY... here is ONE good example: Angulo-Barroso and colleagues (2011) were studying motor development:

Both big stuff, like grabbing a ball...

... and little stuff, like pincer grasp of smaller objects.

← cheerio

They looked at 9-month-old babies across cultures

All the grabby stuff is important 👉 because this skill allows babies to grasp and understand objects.

It is also a BIG part of early social interactions & visual, and cognitive growth. It's pretty huge, as baby skills go.

The researchers focused on 9-month-olds as according to developmental "ages & stages" this is the point when babies BEGIN STANDING AND GRASPING SKILLFULLY.

BUT *culture* also has a hand in things. 🖐

The researchers found that African infants had precocious skills in this area—probably because of care practices that emphasize early sitting and standing.

CULTURE → DEVELOPMENT

Super (1976) found similarly— Kipsigis babies in Western Kenya were part of a group whose cultural care practices influenced the babies' developmental trajectory. It differed from what "*ages & stages*" dictates.

The Kipsigis practices emphasized the value of babies' sitting UPRIGHT. So, babies were placed in special padded holes and propped up with blankets to help them "sit up."

These babies learned to sit up LONG before European or American babies for whom no "sitting ritual" was practiced.

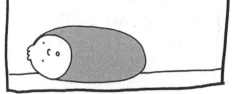

While the Kipsigis and other babies were typically ahead of stage theory AND Western babies, the Western babies did eventually catch up.

The point is, the Kipsigis babies weren't abnormal—nor were the Western babies. The rigid stage model is the problem.

Rather, the practices associated with child care drove a developmental timetable.

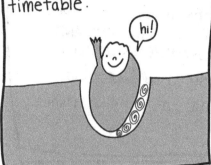

So, while Western babies usually have delays in gross motor development compared with African babies.

This isn't because they are delayed. Rather, we can look at _cultural_ practices.

For example, in contexts with very protective child care cultures — like the U.S. and Japan — mothers carry babies or keep them contained a lot of the time.

baby's so safe in the baby bouncer!

and that baby gets less free floor play, and so also slower gross motor development.

So safe in mama's arms.

I get it! So, my nephew had this weird flat head because he was made to sleep on his back as an infant...

Flat

BABY

Well — that's not really _development_...

No... but it is relevant! Hold on a minute

My brother took my baby nephew to the doctor, and asked about the baby's head.

Wow. That is a very flat head.

The flatness, or POSITIONAL PLAGIOCEPHALY, is an abnormality the doctor was seeing a lot of recently... and it was driven by a change in cultural child care practices. sigh.

This was because in the early 1990's, doctors and others told parents to place their babies ON THEIR BACKS for sleeping.

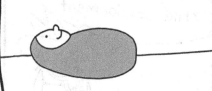

Before this shift in baby care practice, folk wisdom dictated putting babies to sleep on their stomachs.

Babies slept soundly and were supposedly prevented from aspirating their own secretions.

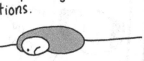

But it was also connected to Sudden Infant Death Syndrome. After the "back to sleep" campaign, American babies started exhibiting less Sudden Infant Death Syndrome, but much more positional plagiocephaly.

So, S.I.D.S. deaths went WAY down.

sounds like a pretty good trade off!

Now HERE is the part about development.

let's hear it!

So, parents then started to notice that their infants were not able to push themselves up onto their arms and lift their heads — not having time on their tummies was cutting off an avenue for development.

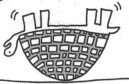

The less time babies spent on their tummies, working to lift heads, etc., the slower they were to acquire a range of motor skills.

Lifting head, rolling over, standing, crawling and eventually walking were all slower in back-sleeping babies, and these differences persisted as far out as six months of age.

getting bored here...

So, the cultural practice and even merchandizing of "tummy time" began in much of the western parenting universe.

"Tummy time" pillow

"Tummy time" play mat

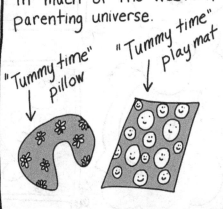

He's a stone cold, child-beating, deficit-thinker bent on salvation through asceticism.

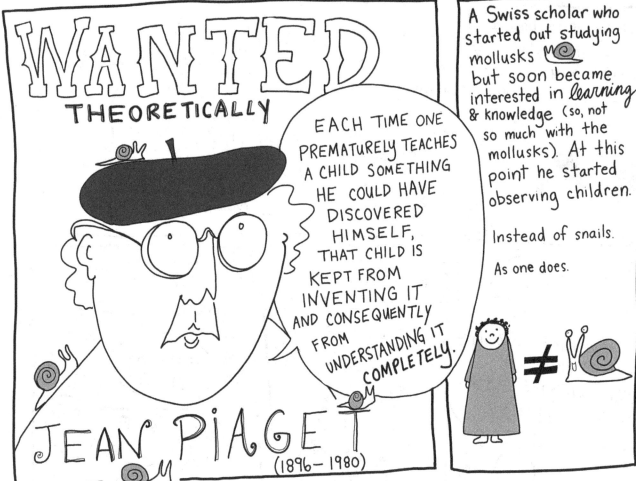

WANTED
THEORETICALLY

EACH TIME ONE PREMATURELY TEACHES A CHILD SOMETHING HE COULD HAVE DISCOVERED HIMSELF, THAT CHILD IS KEPT FROM INVENTING IT AND CONSEQUENTLY FROM UNDERSTANDING IT COMPLETELY.

JEAN PIAGET
(1896 – 1980)

A Swiss scholar who started out studying mollusks but soon became interested in *learning* & knowledge (so, not so much with the mollusks). At this point he started observing children.

Instead of snails.

As one does.

After much time observing Swiss children, he developed "STAGES OF THE DEVELOPMENT OF SWISS CHILDREN," LATER GENERALIZED TO ALL CHILDREN AS "THE STAGES OF COGNITIVE DEVELOPMENT."

STAGES of ~~SWISS~~ COGNITIVE DEVELOPMENT by J.P.

STAGE One =
Sensorimotor
(roughly age birth → 2)

THIS IS DEFINED BY MOSTLY ANIMAL REFLEXES, GRADUALLY MOVING TO "OBJECT PERMANENCE" → e.g.

"if Teddy goes under a blanket he is still there."

STAGE Two =
Preoperational
(roughly age 2-7 years)

CHILDREN HERE USE SYMBOLS TO STAND FOR EVENTS AND

RAHR!

I'm a bear!

OBJECTS IN THEIR LIVES, BUT CANNOT DO FORMAL OPERATIONS LIKE MATH, ETC.

The PREOPERATIONAL STAGE is also a time when children move from EGOCENTRISM to INTUITION.

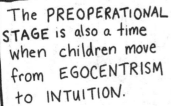

IF I LIKE CHOCOLATE SO DOES EVERYONE ELSE ON THE PLANET.

STAGE *Three*: *Concrete Operational*

(roughly ages 7→12)

children can now REASON LOGICALLY AND APPLY COGNITIVE OPERATIONS to *new thinking.* However, this reasoning is mostly with CONCRETE stuff— NOT with ABSTRACT CONCEPTS. One important skill children develop is <u>CONSERVATION</u>:

STRING A & STRING B = THE SAME LENGTH!

STAGE *Four*: *Formal Operational*

(roughly age 11→ beyond)

This is typically when abstract thinking begins— and HIGHER ORDER REASONING too. At this stage, children can begin to work out PROBLEMS in their HEADS without having to draw a picture.

Hmmm

$$(4+3) \div 6 = \\ 8+1-x +y\sqrt{9} \\ +30\cdots$$

PIAGET is an heir of ROUSSEAU → He also believed that the CHILD is a COMPLETE PERSON— not just a partially-formed adult.

However, PIAGET also saw the CHILD as DEVELOPING INDEPENDENT OF CONTEXT OR CULTURE.

SWISS CHILD in 1900 ? KAYAN CHILD in 1990 =

PIAGET'S ideas were hugely influential in so many ways— For example, they paved the way for things like EXPERIENTIAL LEARNING, Based on Piaget's concept of *Constructivism*

experiences + ideas = KNOWLEDGE

WANTED THEORETICALLY

WANTED THEORETICALLY

Heirs of LOCKE, these fellows believe EVERYTHING is a PRODUCT of EXTERNAL STIMULI

JOHN WATSON (1878 – 1958)

&

B.F. SKINNER (1904–1990)

Watson is the "FATHER OF BEHAVIORISM". A former high school delinquent, he was interested in experimenting on children. Well-known for conducting cruel behavior-modification experiments on a small child called "LITTLE ALBERT" (1925) during which the infant was tortured with rats, iron bars, and hammers. At its most basic, BEHAVIORISM puts children at the same level as lab rats. Watson is on record saying that children should never be kissed or hugged. Not my favorite person.

Picked up Watson's model of behavioral control and developed a model of operant conditioning in which children are TRAINED, like rats or dogs, to exhibit desired BEHAVIORS. Was interested in creating a perfect human species, and believed that one could TRAIN a child to do ANYTHING with conditioning, and didn't really see anything morally questionable in all of it. He remains a favorite of dog owners and mean teachers. Not quite so celebrated and loved by proponents of free will and human dignity.

WANTED

THEORETICALLY

The propensity to make strong emotional bonds to particular individuals is a basic component of human nature.

JOHN BOWLBY (1907–1990)

He developed an idea called **Attachment Theory**

from observations of babies and their primary carers. Bowlby noticed <u>VERY CLOSE</u> <u>BONDS</u> between babies and their carers, who were usually their mothers. ♡♡♡♡♡

He called those strong bonds "ATTACHMENTS" and he posited that they are a key and important requirement for an infant's normal social and emotional development.

ATTACHMENT TO MOTHER IS ALSO PART OF BASIC SURVIVAL.

Attachment theory is important because it emphasizes HUMAN CONNECTION and it asserts that we need CONTACT or even LOVE in order to develop, and that we are pre-programmed to NEED OTHERS.

Reminds me a bit of Rousseau.

It's a LITTLE bit controversial, though, because it has often been used to PATHOLOGIZE diverse parenting and family structures, especially non-Western ones. ☺

WANTED
THEORETICALLY
WHAT A CHILD CAN DO WITH ASSISTANCE TODAY, SHE WILL BE ABLE TO DO BY HERSELF TOMORROW
THROUGH OTHERS WE BECOME OURSELVES.
LEV VYGOTSKY
(1896-1934)
The Russian founder of SOCIOCULTURAL THEORY in human development, VYGOTSKY is a HUGE DEAL.
V
He took developmental theory even FURTHER out of the "Child-Develops-All-Alone" box by suggesting that CULTURE AND HUMAN RELATIONSHIPS DRIVE LEARNING AND DEVELOPMENT!
Similar to Piaget with his emphasis on EXPERIENCE,
Here are some new toys.
?
... but DIFFERENT because he focused on adult help, or SCAFFOLDING, at just the right MOMENT (the cusp of LEARNING a NEW TASK – ALSO KNOWN AS THE ZONE OF PROXIMAL DEVELOPMENT
see?
This helps children learn NEW TASKS!
DEVELOPMENT (& LEARNING) IS A SOCIAL ACTIVITY!
And PLAY is also very important in learning together!

That seems like a LOT of guys named "JOHN." And also two Russians.

But I can see the CONNECTIONS... and how ideas move from a "child alone" view toward perspectives that incorporate the cultural context.

That was also a lot of psychology— Aren't other disciplines chiming in?

All true! But for right now you need to see this GENERAL scaffolding—it's where lots of thinking-- and critiques-- begin. We need to be familiar with these big ideas and how they evolved...

...If we want to interrogate ways of thinking and researching about children. As anthropologist Robert Levine puts it, there is a TRICKY RELATIONSHIP between developmental psychology and the anthropology of childhood.

UNIVERSAL PATTERNS ? CULTURE AND CONTEXT ARE DRIVERS

I feel like I am back at SQUARE ONE.

"NORMAL"

Lots of thinkers and others assert that "ages and stages" thinking distracts us from a more holistic way of thinking about childhood by being too <u>normative</u>...

and by pathologizing children who do not appear to be developing in the same way as others.

SIGH

Everyone wants to bend the conversation toward equity and dignity,

With less focus on what is and isn't "normal".

Yes!

Some thinkers take their critiques a step further.

"These theories are from a white western context, featuring white men and white children. It's set up so that it is possible for any child who is NOT white and western to appear as ABNORMAL by these standards."

see also: COLONIALISM!

So, another case of "take it in context" and with a dash of "western white people wrote this to make themselves look good."

or, adults in perpetual power over children, using theories assuming children's "incomplete development" to oppress and exploit them.

I have to chime in, too! Canella (1997) wrote that a developmentalist perspective, "justifies categorizing children and diverse cultures as backward and needing help from those who are more advanced." (p. 64)

Okay! Let's throw it out!

CHILD DEVELOPMENT
TRASH

NO! keep it!

CHILD DEVELOPMENT
TRASH

child dev

let's just go.

yeah.

I hear you. Let's go back to good old LEVINE & NEW (2008): We need to remember that even though the world is changing, MOST studies of children —even anthropological studies— have been framed using child development theories. BUT we are always in the process of reworking and rethinking all the time.

LEVINE & NEW (2008

"Developmental research has begun to address these questions:" (p.1)

? WHAT does CHILDHOOD look like in different places?

? Are there differences in children's development in different CONTEXTS?

Both Anthropology and Developmental Psychology are quite invested in less normative, more cross-cultural research to answer these very questions.

ANTH ♥ PSYCH

Okay, now can you answer the question: WHAT IS A CHILD?

Well, I COULD, but an answer would be COMPLEX, DYNAMIC and FULL of contradiction, and would take a long time...

...CERTAINLY much more complex than I thought BEFORE I visited this museum!

While Shane is in the gift shop, You have some HOMEWORK!

1. READ AND REFLECT: Find a study that presents a cross-cultural critique of "ages and stages" frames. What was the central critique? What do you learn?

GREAT! Now you can visit the gift shop before we go!

Yes!

2. JOURNAL: What are some of YOUR assumptions about children? Are you more of a LOCKE, ROUSSEAU, or WESLEY?

Chapter Three

THE WILD BUNCH

"Know Your Ethnographers of Childhood"

So, THIS WAS HUGE. FRANZ WENT ON FROM THERE TO ARGUE THAT **CULTURAL** ELEMENTS CAN INFLUENCE ALL KINDS OF DEVELOPMENT INCLUDING COGNITIVE DEVELOPMENT

HE NOTED THAT THIS WAS BECAUSE OF HUMAN

PLASTICITY
&
NEOTENY

DICTIONARY

"PLASTICITY" means we adapt EASILY.

"NEOTENY" means that we mature S L O W L Y.

What is WRONG with you? How old are you again? I am FOUR months old and I can already lick my own butt.

Also, there is a WIDE range of normal variation in human development.

So, cultural, social, environmental and other forces have time and fertile ground in which to work.

You can read more about all of this in

Boas, F. (1911). "Instability of human types." in G.W. Stocking (ed.) 1974. A Franz Boas Reader 1883-1911. New York; Basic Books. p214-218.

AMONG SAMOANS, CHILDREN WERE TREATED AS ADULTS-IN-TRAINING WITH A TOTALLY DIFFERENT STYLE OF PLAY.

"SAMOAN CHILDREN HAVE NO DOLLS, NO PLAY HOUSES, NO TEA SETS, NO TOY BOATS FOR DOLLS. THEY HAVE REAL BABIES. AT 6 THEY ARE EXPECTED TO SWEEP UP THE REAL HOUSE..."

"...LITTLE BOYS ANXIOUS TO BECOME REAL BOATMEN PADDLE ABOUT IN CANOES WITHIN THE SAFETY OF THE LAGOON." (1928)

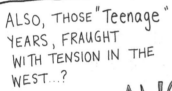

ALSO, THOSE "TEENAGE" YEARS, FRAUGHT WITH TENSION IN THE WEST...?

NOW SHOWING: TEEN ANGST!

AAAGH!

REBEL

MY PARENTS ARE SO STUPID!

I HATE EVERYONE!

NOT A PART OF SAMOAN ADOLESCENCE!

Samoan teen not experiencing angst.

IT WAS A CULTURAL NOT DEVELOPMENTAL HAPPENING!

IT'S NOT FAIR WHY CAN'T I BE SAMOAN?!?

AND WITHIN THESE OBSERVATIONS WAS A CRITIQUE OF PIAGET...

...SUGGESTING HIS STAGES WERE NOT QUITE AS UNIVERSAL AS PROPONENTS CLAIMED (1932)

Look! Imaginary fairies!

PIAGET'S SWISS CHILDREN MAY HAVE THOUGHT ONE WAY, BUT THAT DOESN'T MEAN ALL CHILDREN DO.

You Swiss kids are so weird with your animistic thought.

WITH RICH, THICKLY DESCRIPTIVE FIELD WORK IN THE TROBRIANDS (so very rich that people were quite surprised and amazed)

HE PROVIDED AN ETHNOGRAPHIC ACCOUNT OF YOUTH IN THAT CONTEXT WHICH CONTESTED WIDELY ACCEPTED FREUDIAN IDEAS ON PSYCHO-SEXUAL DEVELOPMENT.

... INCLUDING THE SUPPOSED UNIVERSALITY OF THE OEDIPUS COMPLEX.

HE ILLUSTRATED THAT THESE SUPPOSED UNIVERSALS WERE CULTURALLY & CONTEXTUALLY INFORMED AND DEPENDENT.

NO OEDIPUS COMPLEX IN THE TROBRIANDS!

HE ALSO DESCRIBED A CULTURE WHERE FATHERS CARED FOR THEIR INFANTS

HI DAD

AND CHILD CARE WAS NOT "INNATE" ONLY TO WOMEN, BUT WHERE PARENTING ROLES WERE CULTURALLY INFORMED.

CHILD CARE IN MATRIARCHAL TROBRIAND SOCIETY GAVE EVERYONE NEW WAYS TO BE CRITICAL WESTERN PATRIARCHY.

You can read my 1929 paper, "The Sexual Life of Savages" if you promise to forgive me for the really quite offensive title. It was 1929.

I'M MEYER FORTES, A BRITISH SOUTH AFRICAN YOU'VE PROBABLY NEVER HEARD OF BUT YOU WILL GET TO KNOW ME! (1906–1983)

...THEIR CULTURAL CONTEXT, THEIR LEARNING ACTIVITIES, ROUTINES AND EXPECTATIONS.

MY WORK ON THE TALLENSI PEOPLE OF GHANA IS CLASSIC CHILDHOOD WORK. I LOOKED CAREFULLY AT THE LIVES OF TALLENSI CHILDREN.

I MADE A PORTRAIT OF HOW CHILDREN LEARN IN A NON-WESTERN CONTEXT, CHALLENGING NORMATIVE WESTERN IDEA OF HOW LEARNING "SHOULD" HAPPEN.

What is this MADNESS? Learning only happens at a DESK!!

MINE WAS ALSO AMONG THE FIRST ETHNOGRAPHIES TO METICULOUSLY LOOK AT THE LIVES OF CHILDREN, THEIR GAMES AND TOYS, AND THEIR LIVES AS MORE THAN MERELY PERIPHERAL TO ADULT GOINGS-ON.

I am worthy of focused study!

I EVEN LEARNED HOW TO MAKE CLAY ANIMALS FOR THEM TO PLAY WITH.

I LEARNED HOW EVEN VERY SMALL CHILDREN RESPOND TO CHALLENGES AND NEW INFORMATION.

YOU CAN READ MY MANY BOOKS AND PAPERS ABOUT THE TALLENSI BUT THE BEST IS PROBABLY

The Web of Kinship (1949)

I'M RUTH BENEDICT

...AND NOT A SIGN OF PATHOLOGY, AND THAT CULTURE AND DEVELOPMENT ARE CONNECTED.

Culture ⟷ development

I PUSHED FOR ACADEMICS AND OTHERS TO SEE THAT *Cultural Variation* IN HOW CHILDREN DEVELOP IS TO BE EXPECTED.

MY BOOK, *PATTERNS OF CULTURE* (1934) AND MY PAPER "CONTINUITIES AND DISCONTINUITIES IN CULTURAL CONDITIONING" (1938) SERVE TO DISRUPT THE NORMATIVITY OF WESTERN IDEAS.

FOR EXAMPLE:

"FROM A COMPARATIVE POINT OF VIEW, OUR CULTURE GOES TO GREAT EXTREMES IN EMPHASIZING CONTRASTS BETWEEN THE CHILD AND THE ADULT..."

CHILD SPACE

BIG HUGE GULF

ADULT SPACE

" ... THE CHILD IS SEXLESS, THE ADULT ESTIMATES HIS VIRILITY BY HIS SEXUAL ACTIVITIES, THE CHILD MUST BE PROTECTED FROM THE UGLY FACTS OF LIFE, THE ADULT MUST MEET THEM WITHOUT PSYCHIC CATASTROPHE; THE CHILD MUST OBEY, THE ADULT MUST COMMAND THIS OBEDIENCE..."

Those Americans have some strange ideas.

" ... THESE ARE ALL DOGMAS OF OUR CULTURE, DOGMAS WHICH, IN SPITE OF THE FACTS OF NATURE, OTHER CULTURES COMMONLY DO NOT SHARE. (1955, p. 21-22)

who raises their kids this way?

The "WAY WE DO THINGS" isn't REAL in a BIOLOGICALLY imperative sense, or as PHYSIOLOGICAL truth.

These are all merely "CULTURAL ACCRETIONS" (1955, p. 22)

IT WAS A BIG DEAL TO MAKE A DISTINCTION BETWEEN A "CULTURAL ACCRETION" AND A "PROPER METHOD OF CHILD-REARING"

MIND = BLOWN

"THUS, FROM 1928 TO 1950, PROFESSIONAL ANTHROPOLOGISTS LED BY MEAD AND MALINOWSKI CREATED AN ANTHROPOLOGY OF CHILDHOOD THAT WAS GROUNDED IN ETHNOGRAPHIC FIELDWORK IN DIVERSE CULTURES AND CRITICAL OF DEVELOPMENTAL FORMULATIONS IN PSYCHOLOGY..."

"... THEY CONSTRUCTED CONCEPTS TO STUDY THE CHILD'S ACQUISITION OF CULTURE THE COLLECTION OF ETHNOGRAPHIC DATA ON CHILDHOOD — IN RELATION TO KINSHIP, RELIGION, THE FAMILY THE LIFE CYCLE, AND OTHER STANDARD ETHNOGRAPHIC TOPICS, AS WELL AS PSYCHOLOGICAL DEVELOPMENT— BECAME PART OF THE ETHNOGRAPHER'S CONVENTIONAL TOOLKIT."
(Levine, 2007 p. 253)

WOW. That was weird. They can do a voiceover all the way out here?

I'll say it — I HAVE met some of you before but I didn't know you worked in CHILDHOOD!

We DO! Most anthropologists have historically ignored kids

Well... they just ignored us as peripheral but not totally important...

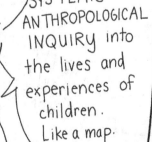
They did — but WE didn't! And we can help you see how larger trends led to a more SYSTEMIC ANTHROPOLOGICAL INQUIRY into the lives and experiences of children. Like a map.

YAY! A TREASURE MAP!
Uh... Kind of...

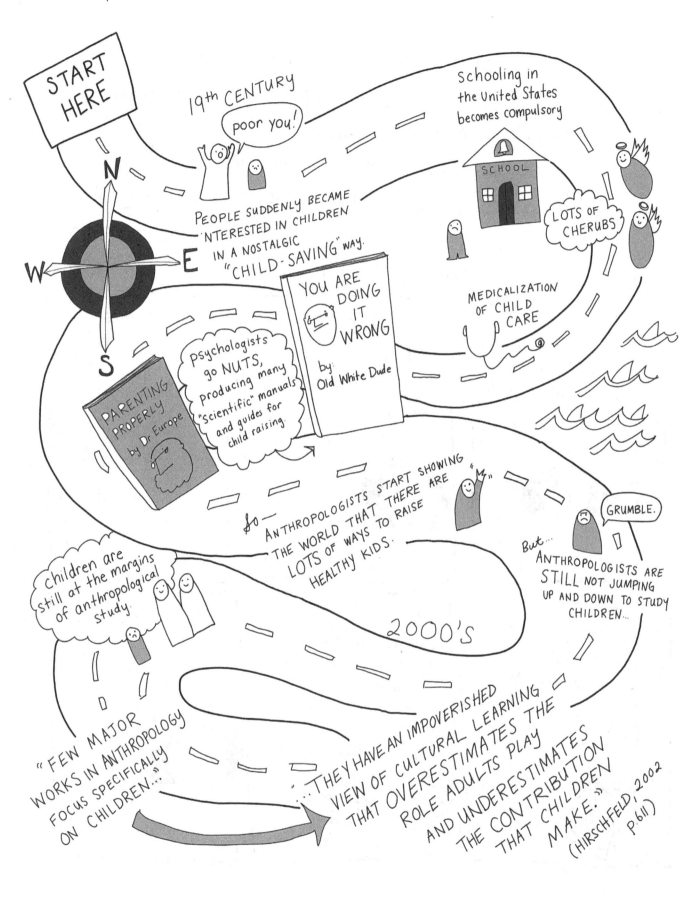

FRONT ········> cut and fold! BACK

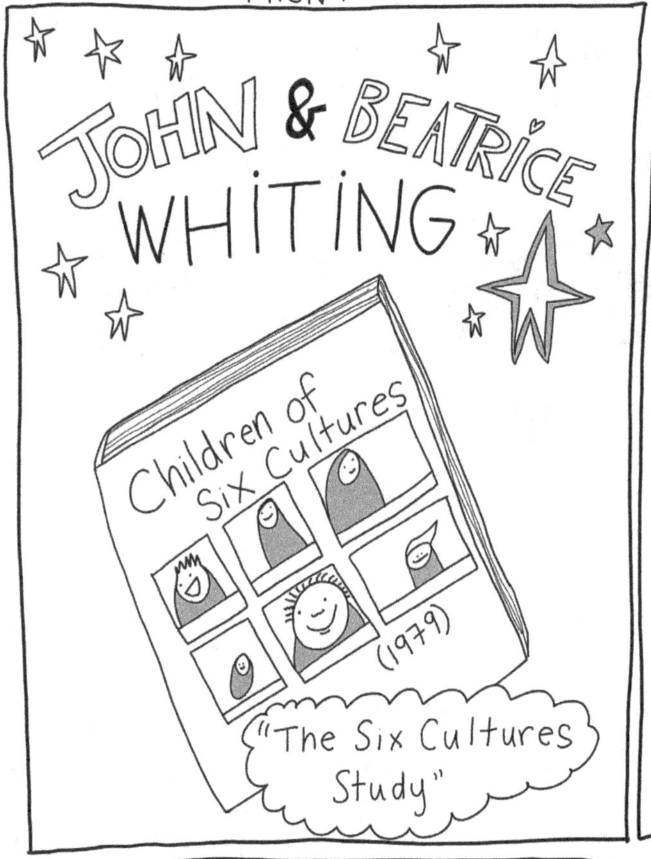
JOHN & BEATRICE
WHITING
Children of Six Cultures
(1979)
"The Six Cultures Study"

- A very structured comparative ethnographic project, which collected RICH data from six cultures.
- was carefully designed to generate comparable data from diverse cultures on *child rearing practices*
- Basically the first time anyone had conducted a systematic scientific and naturalistic observational study of children.
- Really raised the bar for how we do ethnographic field work on childhood.

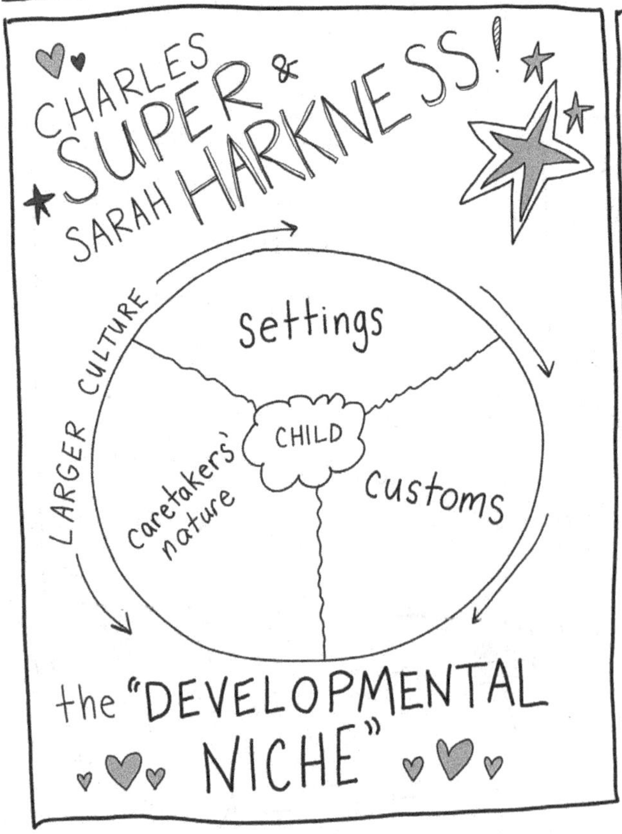
CHARLES SUPER & SARAH HARKNESS!
LARGER CULTURE
settings
CHILD
caretakers' nature
customs
the "DEVELOPMENTAL NICHE"

- Came up with idea that culture shapes development AKA, the "developmental niche" concept.
- places the child as the center of a dynamic system.
- the child's development is shaped by their personality and environment.
- the settings of social life, customs and nature of caregiver make up the niche itself.

BARBARA ROGOFF

THE CULTURAL NATURE OF HUMAN DEVELOPMENT (2003)

★ A developmentalist, she is an heir of VYGOTSKY and a BRIDGE builder.

★ Replaced antiquated terms and thinking about socialization with theory of "guided participation," to show that children learn about their world by interacting with others and being guided by them.

★ We learn with help from more knowledgeable others.

DAVID LANCY

PLAYING ON THE MOTHERGROUND (1996)

✴ Anthropological work on play was groundbreaking in the late 20th century.

✴ Focused on lots of different kinds of play, Playing on the Motherground (1996) examines child development via a careful look at play.

✴ Kpelle children in West Africa play in open spaces where adults work, and become enculturated by watching adults, playing games and otherwise engaging on "the motherground."

DELL HYMES

☆ work on language acquisition and communication, focusing on language, identity and the ethnographic study of speech and social & cultural relations.

☆ "Communicative competence" means that WE USE MORE THAN WORDS TO COMMUNICATE

Reinventing Anthropology
AND A MILLION OTHER BOOKS
(1974)

"a child acquires knowledge of sentences not only as grammatical, but also as appropriate. He or she acquires competence as to when to speak, when not, and as to what to talk about with whom, when, where, in what manner ... a child becomes able to accomplish a repertoire of speech acts." (1972, p.277)

Barrie THORNE

★ a sociologist who accounted for how children divide themselves and how they are grouped by gender

★ This ethnographic work disrupts essentialist claims about gender with years of intense fieldwork in elementary school.

★ Found that boys and girls do "border work," which is the reinforcement work of making boundaries between themselves using real and imagined things — like "cooties" and chasing games, but also quietly and agentively breaking down boundaries.

Kids are agents!

GENDER PLAY: Boys & Girls in School (1993)

IONA & PETER OPIE

The People in the Playground (1994)

The Lore and Language of Schoolchildren (1965)

★ primarily children's folklorists

★ worked extensively to document and understand children's culture and the folklore of childhood.

★ used ethnographic methods to contest the idea that modern life was "ruining" children's folklore traditions and games.

★ Iona's later work featured meticulous data collection in playground settings to faithfully portray children at play.

★ Was the first effort to record children's playground culture as it happened

JOHN OGBU

Black American Students in an Affluent Suburb (2003)

Minority Education & Caste (1978)

★ Comparative ethnographic work on minority education for three decades.

★ Used ethnographic work with Black American children to provide a deep understanding of educational inequality, racism and the experiences of Black students in public schools.

★ Argued that Black American youth were part of a "caste-like minority" and that this had a deleterious effect on their opportunity to learn. The first to make these observations, Ogbu is an intellectual giant.

ANNETTE Laureau

Unequal childhoods: Race, class & family life (2003)

★ indepth ethnography examines how class makes an impact in the lives of American children.

★ observations of black and white children from a range of socioeconomic classes reveal different patterns of childrearing.

★ middle class families engage in "concerted cultivation" to draw out children's talents.

★ Working class and poor families rely on "the accomplishment of natural growth" — allowing a child's development to follow naturally, without intervention.

★ BOTH approaches have advantages.

ALMA GOTTLIEB

The Afterlife is Where we come From (2004)

★ A pioneer in the field of ethnography of infancy, she puts the life of babies front and center.

★ When a baby is born to the Beng people of Africa, they are not new people but instead reincarnated beings from the afterlife.

★ The belief in babies' rich internal and spiritual lives makes child care and child life unique.

SARADA ★ **BALAGOPALAN**

Inhabiting "Childhood": Children, Labour and Schooling in Post-Colonial India

(2014)

★ Explores and meticulously documents the lives of street children and child laborers in Calcutta.

★ Goes beyond the frame of multiple childhoods to explore the "victimized" child from a critical postcolonial lens.

★ Focuses on the experiences of the child in the midst of intervention and the tensions between work and schooling.

★ ANN ARNETT ★ **FERGUSON**

BAD BOYS: Public Schools in the Making of Black Masculinity

(2001)

★ Ethnographic work spanning three years at an elementary school, looks carefully at the lives and experiences of Black boys in school.

★ Theorizes powerfully about the criminalization of Black children by the adults in schools.

★ Focuses on the perspectives of the children themselves to document their agency in the face of unfair treatment and racism.

★ Deconstructs the term "at risk" and all that goes with it...

BAMBI CHAPIN

Childhood in a Sri Lankan Village (2014)

★ A careful look at socializing process among toddlers and young children rural Sri Lankan contexts.

★ Chapin tracked the children's development and cultural acquisition through a decade of observing small everyday interaction.

★ Presents an ethnographic account of evolving village life through the eyes of the youngest children over time, with an eye toward enculturation in a Buddhist belief system..

BRIAN SUTTON-SMITH

Folkstories of Children (1981)

The Ambiguity of Play (2001)

★ In his *New York Times* obituary Sutton-Smith was called the "scholar of what's fun."

★ A developmental psychologist, he focused on (play) from the children's perspective, capturing their voices telling stories and playing games.

★ Not actually *ethnographic*, per se, but important bridging work for interdisciplinary study in childhood.

★ Transformative theory for any scholar!

★ one of the groundbreaking modern ethnographers of childhood.

★ Falls in the tradition of the ethnography of child-rearing practices.

★ The first systematic account of growing up in Tonga spanning pregnancy and birth through late childhood and early adolescence.

★ To "become Tongan", a child must move from a state of social incompetence to one of social competence, marked by very specific cultural knowledge.

★ Ethnography of literacy development via in-depth fieldwork in an urban U.S. first grade classroom.

★ Focuses on the children's culture and their lives, and how these may be circumscribed by school practices.

★ Focal children's "landscape of voices" reflects how they agentively move through social spaces.

★ These "textual toys" – like jump rope songs, movies and TV – and all the voices at play influence their literacy activities.

Homework

While Shane is READING and READING and R E A D I N G here is some *homework* for (YOU)!

1. Have a look in the appendix and review the "trading cards" from this chapter.

2. Pick ONE book-length ethnography of childhood

3. Read the whole thing! Enjoy!

4. Reflect: What makes this an ethnography? What is it saying about children? About CONTEXT? Which work(s) is it building on? Which traditions?

BONUS ➡ Make your own trading cards to supplement this chapter.

Chapter Four

GET ALONG LITTLE DOGIES:

An Introduction to Method

3. MULTIPLE CHILDHOODS

Childhood environments vary across material, social and cultural conditions. All childhoods are "normal" and "count" as childhoods.

Childhood happens in CONTEXT → NOT as an independent variable.

A very fancy triangle of context

material: "stuff" and setting

social: Relationships and how people organize themselves and interact.

cultural: shared meaning-making systems and norms.

4. PARENTING HAPPENS IN CONTEXT TOO!

There is no ONE universal "right" or "wrong" way to parent. What is good parenting in one cultural context may be "bad" parenting in a different one.

5. CHILDREN ARE NOT SPONGES.

I know... you have heard this before BUT it is very IMPORTANT to remember that children learn and create and teach and curate what they see and hear around them!

"Children are not passive receivers of cultural practice. They acquire the conventions of communication and norms of behavior that give the entrée into their local and social world, but they use and modify them for their own purpose."

Levine & New 2008 p. 3

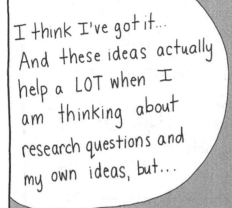

I think I've got it... And these ideas actually help a LOT when I am thinking about research questions and my own ideas, but...

But what?

But I guess I still have questions about the NUTS & BOLTS of method.

Like, do I just walk up to a kid and start asking questions?

Uh... probably not.

Well, we haven't even gotten started! Get ready for some HANDS-ON PRACTICAL direction!

The "nuts and bolts" are always informed by the "big idea" stuff. (And vice versa!)

Methods are a big topic, but we can get started with THREE DRIVING ASSUMPTIONS from Graue & Walsh (1998 p.57)

1. ALL KIDS ARE SMART.

2. ALL KIDS MAKE SENSE.

3. ALL KIDS WANT TO HAVE A GOOD LIFE.

driving? get it? ☺

Our buddies Graue & Walsh (1998) break it down for us!

1. <u>ALL</u> kids are SMART.

"the only way to get as smart as they are about their world is to learn from them."
(p. 99)

So, if I dismiss a child's talk or play or behavior as silly or senseless I am in fact missing out on data and being a thoughtless researcher?

Yes.

2. ALL KIDS MAKE SENSE.

Kids do everything for a REASON.
You, as an adult, just may not be able to see it.
Before you decide something doesn't make "sense" - consider that you don't understand.

3. ALL kids want to have a good life.

Kids are STRATEGIC about this and are tireless in their pursuit of this goal. Just because you can't or won't see it does not mean it is not there. It is purposeful.

Be CRITICAL of your view from the OUTSIDE, especially if you think you are seeing something "dysfunctional" or "destructive." (p. 99)

OW!   PINCH!

... because from the INSIDE it isn't. It makes SENSE.

It may not be aligned with your adultist ideas about cherubic behavior, but it is SMART and STRATEGIC.

That is my bear.

No. I have it.

This reminds me of something else I read... the idea of "GENEROUS CONSTRUCTION."

YEEHAW! Run with it!

It's an idea from Martha Nussbaum (1995) — the notion that we should construct things and others generously... we should see the possibility not just the seeming appearances, loaded down with our own baggage.

WOW. All that reading for my PhD DID pay off!

Anyway, I found the book! Here's what Nussbaum writes: "Here we see all the abilities of fancy, deftly woven together: its ability to endow a perceived form with rich and complex significance, its GENEROUS CONSTRUCTION of the seen." (p. 43)

POETIC JUSTICE

Martha Nussbaum

"Fancy" is kind of a big idea here.

FANCY

Nussbaum writes that FANCY allows us to dream the POSSIBLE through "its preference for WONDER over pat solutions; its playful and surprising moments... this imagination is necessary. With it, reason is beneficent, steered by a generous view of its objects; without its charity, reason is cold and cruel."

(p. 43)

"this is even more personal than theoretical frameworks or disciplinary traditions — it includes personal experience, memory, identity, and society... we see children in our work through prisms of our own memory, ... and hopeful emotions for the future." (74)

Children often see female adults as either mothers or teachers.

MOTHER   TEACHER

To try to adopt a different role, THORNE became the "ADULT VISITOR." (1993)

NOT a teacher or a mom.

THORNE writes, "I claimed the free-lancing privilege of an adult visitor. I could, and did, come and go, shift groups...

She's not a teacher. Look! She is leaving the room.

... choose and alter my daily routines. Unlike the kids, I was relatively, although not entirely, free from the control of the principals, teachers, and aides...

...and she can't be a KID because she can do what she WANTS.

... without a fixed school-based routine, I also had more spatial mobility than the teachers or aides." (p. 14)

Hmmm... she must be a DIFFERENT kind of adult? A VISITOR?

However, even an adult visitor, and a thoughtful, reactive adult, is still an ADULT. How should one negotiate these boundaries?

FRIEND
ADULT

FINE & SANDSTROM'S (1988) "ADULT FRIEND" role blends adult authority with friendly rapport.

I acknowledge that I'm an adult. But I am a friendly and friend-like one!

and I maintain an adult identity!

I don't have teacher or parent "authority," but I also don't try to erase the obvious gulf of power and responsibility.

I can still have access to the world(s) of children, develop friendly rapport, and respect this BOUNDARY.

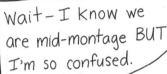

Wait— I know we are mid-montage BUT I'm so confused.

A lot of this sounds like I need to be an adult but also NOT an adult. HOW?!?

Imagine you are six years old. What are your ideas about what adults do?

SHANE! PUT THAT THING DOWN! STOP PINCHING YOUR SISTER! IT'S RUDE TO PICK YOUR NOSE IN PUBLIC! LEAVE THE CAT ALONE! STOP EATING OUT OF THE...

MANDELL (1988) suggests that if you must be an adult, you should take up the "LEAST ADULT" role.

NO NO NO NO DON'T DON'T DON'T NO NO NO N DON'T DON'T NO NO

← MOST adult role.

This can mean that you modify how you perform your adult identity so you are <u>not</u> an authority figure or enforcer of rules.

So, one way of thinking about it is that you don't resolve peer disputes or act as the "law." In this way you minimize the power differential and build trust.

Timmy isn't SHARING!

I'm not a teacher. I am sorry I can't help. Maybe you should talk to the teacher?

MAKE HIM SHARE!

This is easier said than done.

That felt weird and it was hard NOT to help. I feel conflicted. But I also did not invoke adult POWER.

CHRISTENSEN (2004) also thought this was really a challenge, that the power differential is much more COMPLEX... So, rather than be the LEAST adult, you should resolve to be "AN UNUSUAL ADULT."

hi

wow.

The UNUSUAL TYPE OF ADULT is not defined by non-engagement, but rather by INTEREST.

I'm interested in your drawing!

Interest in child perspectives.

I'm interested in what pretend game you are playing!

The one thing the UNUSUAL TYPE OF ADULT is NOT interested in is exercizing AUTHORITY

You need to ask a teacher about that.

Tell Timmy that he HAS TO SHARE!

All these ways of being an adult seem the same but also make a little uncomfortable in different ways.

Well, it is not an easy balance. The role you choose will be both personal and imperfect. It is really about your research and your beliefs,

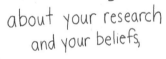

And the adult role you like the best.

?

What will you say on Day One of fieldwork, when:

Hey, who are you?

Are you Keisha's mom?

WHO you are, HOW you interact and WHAT you believe will inform this answer and so much more.

are you a teacher?

Okay - let's say I do my thinking and I'm ready, how do I get started?

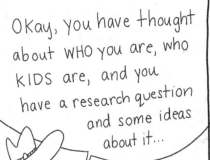

Okay, you have thought about WHO you are, who KIDS are, and you have a research question and some ideas about it...

I have LOTS of ideas! But I don't have a research site and HOW DO I GET ONE?

And NOW it is nuts-and-bolts time?

oh - and do skip ahead to the IRB and ethics chapter right about here!

The Field

Sometimes, researchers know EXACTLY where they want to be.

Or EXACTLY the group that they are interested in.

BUT, as Graue & Walsh observe, doing the fieldwork is often easier than gaining access to the field.

NO ACCESS

TEACHER   MOM   FOSTER PARENT   CAMP DIRECTOR   SPORT COACH

BEHOLD the GATEKEEPERS
(these are just a few)

Gatekeepers are the adults with access to children, who protect children, and who may prevent, delay, ease, or obstruct your attempt to get access to the children & the site.

They are doing their job!

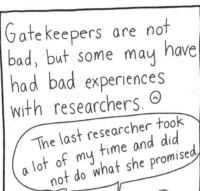

Gatekeepers are not bad, but some may have had bad experiences with researchers. ☹

The last researcher took a lot of my time and did not do what she promised.

Researchers may make some people anxious, too.

It can be difficult for them, and challenging for you— but before you get frustrated...

What am I doing WRONG?!?

CONSIDER ♥ THESE ♥ **TIPS** FOR **RESEARCH ACCESS**

(thanks to Graue & Walsh, p. 98)

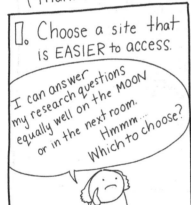

1. Choose a site that is EASIER to access.

I can answer my research questions equally well on the MOON or in the next room. Hmmm... Which to choose?

2. Have all your documentation on hand, but don't drown people in it.

here is a one-page overview with bulleted lists and bold keywords.

3. Find out who the key gatekeepers are and try talking to them first.

NOT THE ONE   NOT ME   YES! ME!

4. Be humble and grateful and do not waste others' time.

I am a Humble LEARNER!

DON'T BE THIS ONE

A BIG & FANCY IMPORTANT RESEARCHER WHO IS BETTER THAN EVERYONE

5. Once you have some access, be a HELPER.

Hey, can I help clean out that art supply closet?

HUMBLE LEARNER

6. Take it slow. Let people get to know you.

Oh look! A nice letter from the researcher I met at the school last week!

Shane has some thinking to do... so, while we are waiting, let's take a minute to MEET a bonafide REAL LIFE GUEST STAR!

hmm... ACCESS?

DR. KATZ-WISE is a SUPER COOL researcher Harvard Medical School & Boston Children's Hospital

DR. SABRA KATZ-WISE!

When I am in the process of entering the community for my project with families with transgender youth, I consider how I am perceived by the community members.

I am a cisgender woman, and I do not yet have children, nor do I have any transgender family members, so I am an OUTSIDER to this community.

INSIDER / OUTSIDER

I don't have experience as a member.

So, I stepped out of the traditional "researcher as expert" role.

Researcher as Learner

Research as Expert

... and into the role of researcher as learner.

I made a conscious choice to enter the community as an ALLY and ADVOCATE with some knowledge of the community BUT to defer almost COMPLETELY to community members as EXPERTS of their own EXPERIENCE

ALLY & ADVOCATE

Conducting research with youth adds another dimension to this approach...

?

I'm in my 30's, and have experience being an adolescent and child, but I don't know what it is like to be a youth in our current socio-historical period.

WE HAT
EVERYON
(especially you

in particular,

meBook

I didn't grow up with SOCIAL MEDIA.

So, again, I begin research with youth assuming they are EXPERTS in their own experience.

click

And, I am careful not to make assumptions about their experiences.

In my current work transgender youth, I use principles of

Community

Based

Participatory

Research

This means seeking FEEDBACK from the youth at each step in the research process, from study design to data collection.

Talking with lots of different people help make sure I am asking the right questions in the right way.

In this process, I learned that transgender youth want to be taken seriously as experts in their own experience.

EXPERT

One of my jobs a researcher is to make sure these under-represented voices are heard.

Chapter Five

ZZzzz zzZZZ

SLEEPING BABIES TELL NO TALES

Listening to Children

Okay. First leave behind your ideas about how it is SUPPOSED to look.

Graue & Walsh (1998) say,

"the purpose of interviews is to get [children] to talk about what they know." (p. 112)

Further, the *Ethnographic* interview is more specialized because we want:

→ children's OWN views on their experience

→ understanding of the cultural foundations that shape those views.

(Saywitz & Camparo, 2014, p. 375)

It is going to look and feel different from adult Q&A. It is working WITH children rather than doing research ON them. (James, 2001)

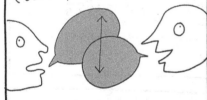

Just as all adults are different, so too all children are different.

It's good to use a variety of approaches to appreciate difference.

AGE?

Cultural context?

language?

experience with adults? which adults?

Research context?

Special needs?

Graue & Walsh (1998) write that most children believe that when an adult asks a question, the adult already knows the answer.

what color is this ball?

"... or that they are in trouble."

What were you thinking when you threw this ball through the window?

"Few children have had the experience of being approached by an adult who wants them, the kids, to teach her, the adult, about their lives."

(p. 113)

Adult ideas of an "interview" sometimes resemble a police procedural drama.

Or, a workplace interaction, or commercial exchange.

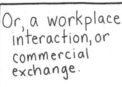

How much is the blah blah blah?

The blah is blah.

Bye then.

and typically do not look much like conversations that are happening among people socially- or among children.

Rossman & Rallis (2017) suggest researchers move away from the Adult Way of Interviewing and instead PLAY with children.

Maybe work a puzzle together, or build with blocks.

Or hang out at snack time and enjoy a nice chat.

The point is that the researcher ENTERS THE CHILDREN'S CONTEXT, ready to listen and to learn.

Rather than the other way around.

Alienating Interview Room.

Transforming the "interview" into a conversation, often while engaged in an activity, puts children at ease. However, be prepared to invest a fair amount of TIME.

2. Interview children in small groups instead of one-on-one

snack time again!

One-on-one might be stressful for children (no matter how nice you are.)

LOOK HOW NICE I AM!!!

And this way also allows you to listen to children talking to _each_ other!

I like to play outside.

But not when it is cold or rainy.

Oh-yeah. Then I like playing blocks.

Children talk more and sometimes differently to other children.

tell me about playing outside.

I like it.

"Interviewing children in groups may also reduce the researcher's power within the research context, because the presence of peers will typically take precedence over the presence of the researcher." (Freeman & Mathison, 2009, p. 88)

Furthermore, group interactions with children can be a lot of FUN — more fun and probably more informative than one-on-one.

Yeah, I guess that I don't always prefer playing outside.

only the grown-ups think that!

3. Focus on getting the children to tell you a STORY. Do not ask Yes/no questions*

FULL OF STORIES!

*This is also just good interviewing!

Asking Yes/No type questions may remind children of the kinds of questions adults ask when they already know the answer.

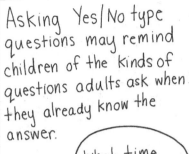

What time are you supposed to go to bed?

Yes/No questions are also not good for getting descriptive information! (from anyone)

DATA
- yes
- no
- yes
- no
- yes
- no
- yes
- yes
- no
- no

?

INSTEAD, ask questions like this:

Tell me about a time when...

Can you give me an example of...

This way you can get a story!

OR

What are the steps you take when you...

OR

Can you tell me about a time when something unexpected happened instead?

Also, by positioning the CHILD as KNOWER in this way, you get rich data <u>and</u> build better rapport.

The adult is listening to ME and learning from ME!

In most contexts, the adults are considered to know more than children do, so in resisting playing into this pattern you can improve your practice and also "remedy children's deference to adult knowledge..."

"...emphasizing that [you] are most interested in what the CHILD remembers and believes." (Saywitz & Camparo, 2014 p. 383)

Sure, Adult power is built into every interview, and it is a larger cultural pattern that we cannot totally shift, but that is no reason to not think deeply about it, or not to TRY to shift it in our work.

Using a story-eliciting approach can help you catch confusing language, too

Have you done shpfclrgrd?

yes... uh, no?

Start with big "tell me a story" kinds of questions. This gives you a chance to see if children are understanding your words, or if you need to rephrase.

Tell me a story about when you shpfclrgrd?

uh... I...

I meant, when you played outside

And gently prompt.

what happened NEXT?

Also, at the end, make sure children get the opportunity to ask questions too.

Do you have any questions for me?

Can you tell me about a time when you played outside?

4 use fun stuff*

o Graue & Walsh (1998) call these things "props."

These can be used to provide something fun to do while a pair or group sit together.

... or they can be tools to help children organize their thinking.

I'll show you! This is what my house looks like.

* within limits - tools should not be distracting...

Props that help children ORGANIZE their thinking can be lots of things.

Like photographs relevant to your questions...

Or laminated pictures and/or cut out numbers, letters & symbols...

... Or dolls or animal or other figurines to act things out.

And even the craft supplies you may already be using for activity during interviews can be employed as tools for organization and expression

play clay

But, again, do NOT get carried away!
Too many props, or poorly thought-out ones, could end up leading the interview or derailing it utterly!

Also, if you are doing more "formal" interviews, or something that takes some time, provide some snacks! (check for allergies)

CHEEZE BLOBZ

5. Graue & Walsh (1998) suggest the use of hypothetical or third-person questions in interviews to make children more comfortable.

What kinds of games do KIDS play outside

"The interviewer makes it clear that she is not trying to delve into the child's privacy.
She is also communicating that she sees the child as an expert on this particular subject." (p.115)

6. Remember that these beings in your midst are CHILDREN.

Small {

Researchers should be WARM, KIND, and SUPPORTIVE, and should take the time to build RAPPORT.

BE <u>NICE</u>.

I want children to feel good about meaningful participation.

Being "NICE" in this context means that if problems arise,

UGH! I cannot get the square peg into the round hole!!!

You should not blame the CHILD.

What a BAD PEG!

I'm actually a very fine peg. It is the <u>hole</u> that is the problem.

You are certainly to blame. Perhaps your study design or interview setup was not done with children's needs in mind. Reflect on these before you label child participants as the "problem."

♡

7. ... AND think very carefully about what to do if things don't work out.

sigh.

Even with the best rapport-building, some children will be shy or not feel comfortable sharing with you. Some may even not want to speak.

Freeman & Mathison (2009) suggest a variety of "icebreakers" to help children feel at ease, BEFORE any interview begins.

brrr!

There are lot icebreaker games BUT you probably want to avoid very physical ones. (it can be difficult to calm down.)

GOOOOOO CRAAAAAY-ZEEEE

WOOOOOO HOOoooooo

Instead, choose drawing or talking games that are non-competitive and won't require a calm-down.

YIPPEE!

uh.. time to sit down and, uh.. interview? Calmly?

WOOOOOOOO....

Freeman & Mathison (2009) recommend Winnicott's (1971) "The Squiggle Game," wherein you draw a squiggly line on a piece of paper and the child turns it into something using their imagination.

look! I made it into a person!

You can do something similar by giving out pipe cleaners and asking children to make a self-portrait, or favorite animal. They may also be used afterward as fidgets!

The point is to create a space where children talk, where they may feel less nervous, and where fun or interesting materials provide an opening for participation.

And ALWAYS have a Plan B up your sleeve in case your ice breaker does not work!

I do not like to draw

I made a giraffe!

But I DREAM of recording devices!

PRETTY PLEASE?

OK—I'm an old softie.

Besides, things have really changed in an era of smart and small recording devices.

Smartphones in particular are familiar to many children.

(but not all— don't make assumptions here.)

With this size & familiarity comes less of the excitement that larger devices generate.

However, those little phones really are not the same as professional tools

This video I recorded at my field site is really shaky and hard to see.

So even though a smartphone is familiar and easy to use, you might end up needing to purchase better equipment if you are serious about recording data.

sob

The general rule is that if you want to use audio or video data you should prepare to spend a little money.

FANCY THING

This is also only one part of the equation. You must also consider the child.

WHAT IS THAT?

FANCY THING

BEEP BEEP BEEP BEEP BEEP

BEFORE introducing your new, unfamiliar recording device, focus once more on rapport.

fig 1. Child   fig 2. Device

Weigh carefully how the equipment you choose may affect your site.

Don't mind me!

Some people do not like being recorded. A child may not be sure how to communicate this feeling, so pay attention to nonverbal cues.

He seems nervous. I'll turn off the camera and put it away.

Fancy equipment can also let you down.

I FORGOT TO PRESS RECORD! NOOOOooo

You might also not pay close attention if you think the device is "getting it"

La la la la la   Amazing data

Let children get comfortable with equipment by letting it sit around for a while. Eventually it will become a fixture.

what device?

Now let's get back to that BABY!

Interviewing a baby isn't really developmentally appropriate, you know.

Really? Some Anthropologists might disagree! They might say that you can't do a one-on-one interview with a baby or a toddler, BUT...

That's a great start— BUT THERE'S MORE!

The Afterlife is where we come from.

by Alma Gottlieb

Gottlieb's (2004) The Afterlife is Where We Come From: The Culture of Infancy in West Africa includes babies as participants!

She sought to understand a culture as it is experienced by babies and toddlers.

CHECK OUT THIS VERY IMPORTANT BABY ETHNOGRAPHY

SERIOUSLY. READ IT RIGHT NOW.

The infants in this context are SPIRITUAL, CULTURAL, SOCIAL, DEVELOPING, VALUED, EVERYDAY BEINGS. Child-rearing practices build on this premise, and the belief that babies come into the world filled with knowledge.

Done reading? Ok! Let's get started.

HOW to interview A BABY

1. Locate baby.

2. Think about what you want to know about culture and infancy.

3. Get attuned to "somatic modes of communication." Gottlieb writes, "Babies' more direct efforts to communicate are frequently accomplished by non-speaking means: with nuanced or not-so-nuanced noises -- gurgles, chortles, clucks, and screams; with facial expressions—smiles and grimaces... (p. 54)

(p.54, continued)

"... arched eyebrows and closed eyes; and of course, with body language - waving hands, kicking legs, arched backs. Indeed, so much communication with babies is inevitably bodily rather than purely verbal."

4. How does the baby fit the larger culture of those around them? Of other babies? Of the people who take care of them?

5. What do babies do in response to the conditions around them?

6. Do babies CHANGE the conditions around them? How?

Consider how much of YOUR communication is not "spoken".

... or what you see in older children's communication.

You might also draw maps of where the babies ARE at your site?

NO BABIES HERE.

IN THE BACK IN A SPECIAL DEVICE.

ALSO IN A DEVICE

WORKY OFFICE BUILDING

SWAAAAAAAAAAAA SCREEEEEEE AAAAAAAAAAAM

WESTERN BABY GUIDE for PARENTS

Well... maybe just this ONCE...

As Gottlieb found in the Beng village in Africa where she studied the babies, there <u>are</u> cultures of infancy.

In this community the culture of infancy included that babies communicated, in varied bodily ways.

Look! The baby is HAPPY!

Adults worked hard to be sure they listened to the babies.

Quickly! The baby is unhappy!

In many Western contexts, adults do not believe babies can communicate at all—and that informs their treatment.

OH, LET HER CRY IT OUT.

WAAAAAAH!

Gottlieb writes that, in Beng culture, "Adults told me that babies are driven to communicate..."

"...BUT THAT ADULTS ARE TOO UNENLIGHTENED TO UNDERSTAND THOSE ATTEMPTS"

(p.53)

Gottlieb truly drops the mic here:

"At a methodological level, our field techniques typically require us to rely rather heavily on chats and interviews. But we won't get much of an answer when we ask a baby to explain, say, the meaning of a prayer, or what kind of dinner is appropriate to serve a boss, or why children are segregated by age in school. All this is beyond an interview with an infant. For babies can't speak—at least not in the language we are taught in fieldwork classes to use in interviews" (p. 52).

LEARN TO LISTEN. It is pretty clear when a baby doesn't like something, or when they do—if you pay attention!

So, if a baby or child is very unhappy while participating in my research, it could mean that they DO NOT agree to be in the study?

YES!

You know, I think I understand why we are talking about babies...

Ah! You have found me out!

MAYBE the care we take in attending to all forms of communication is good practice no matter WHO the participant is?

And thinking about context and also beyond our adultist privileging of the one-on-one interview is a good place to begin to deconstruct how we REALLY listen to, and hear, children!

YES! But what are you WEARING?!

Isn't it great? I really want to engage my child participants! I want the interview to be FUN and also CHILD-FRIENDLY! Kids love clowns!

UH-
WHOA.
STOP.

IXNAY ON THE UNFAY.

Be warm and supportive and genuine but DO NOT BE A CLOWN.

But kids love clowns.

Children know when an an adult is trying too hard to be "fun." They may also find it unsettling.

KA-BLAM!!!

Children do not need things like clowns or balloons to make interaction better or to build rapport—in fact, by trying to be "fun" you may end up creating MORE methodological problems.

OOOoooh! Don't you want to play with the magical mystery sock? WHO KNOWS WHAT IS INSIDE?!?

No. But I do like crayons.

Focus instead on what children in your setting are already doing.

if you quietly color with me, I will answer your questions. I already know how to color.

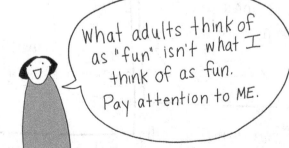

"Child-friendly" means focusing on the child, not on abstract ideas about "children" in general.

What adults think of as "fun" isn't what I think of as fun. Pay attention to ME.

Chapter Six

DANCES WITH TODDLERS

"How to observe children"

Look, I am a hamster who knows what's what. I have been observing children for years. Sit down.

Observation is a central tool in Ethnography.

WOOOOHOOO! LOOK AT ME!

You might be observing in a classroom...

... or outside

... in a home setting

... or at work.

... or anywhere! It's interesting to think of both where children ARE and where they are NOT.

LE FANCY RESTAURANT

The kind of observing we typically do in ethnographic work is

PARTICIPANT OBSERVATION

(it's what makes ethnography tick!)

In Participant Observation, the researcher is seeking to learn about a group by participating in their culture.

I'm getting the hang of it!

Now do it like this.

As an ADULT, the RESEARCHER has a little bit of a complicated participant observation experience ➡️

Adult ≠ child

The children will never accept you as a child.

Hey, I'm a preschooler!

What is wrong with you?

DON'T DO THIS.

This complicates how you might participate in children's culture.

my butt is too big for the swings.

At a dance class, a tea party, or a work setting, you will never BE a child, so your participant observation foregrounds interest, and the search for understanding, but acknowledging that difference.

Keep things open, Be honest, & Learn by participation!

I'm still confused. Does this mean that we are not really fully participating?

Are we really doing semi-participant observation, then? Because we can't really BE children?

YOU ARE SCARING ME DOES THIS MEAN I CAN'T EVER DO THIS KIND OF RESERCH AND NOW WHAT AM I GOING TO

CHILL. OF COURSE YOU CAN DO PARTICIPANT OBSERVATION.

Punch (2002) says maybe we need to reframe what we consider FULL participation. You can participate when self-transformation is not required.

You are learning as a cultural outsider. That's great!

Can you show me how to do that?

There are lots of ways to build trust and rapport, but being an honest and humble learner ...

I want to LEARN

... who is reflective...

If I want to learn about children, what might my participation look like?

... goes a long way.

I like that a grown-up wants to learn what we know!

OKay-so I should NOT pretend to be a child because it isn't honest or authentic.

Right. You would not do that in any other field site, so why pretend with children?

It would be pretty disrespectful, and really, really weird.

Look at me! I am a member of your culture!

It reminds me of when I tried to make research "fun" and "child-friendly" by wearing a clown costume. That felt weird too.

What if we just skip the whole participation thing?

Uh, nope. Participant observation is a cornerstone of ethnography!

Let's zoom back a bit. In childhood ethnography we can learn about the activities and culture of children in lots of ways and develop

UNDERSTANDING

You can PARTICIPATE

You can sit there taking notes (STTN)

BOTH ARE OBSERVATION

But isn't one more, well, ethnographic?

Well, yes...

But we need to think about degrees of participation on a CONTINUUM.

Graue & Walsh (1998) position this as a continuum from:

really involved participant observation (ethnography)

really detached (STTN)

(with lots of places in between)

On one hand, the person doing the detached observation (STTN) "is removed from the children, most often unable to hear clearly what they are saying...

... He cannot ask questions or interact and may be physically limited, too."

(Graue & Walsh p.107)

On the other hand, the really involved participant observer may have difficulty taking careful notes.

"One must rely on short reminder notes as well as 'headnotes' – what one knows from having been there but has not yet been able to write down and then attempt to expand these from memory,

... as the opportunity arises, retreating periodically to an out-of-the-way spot." (p.107)

SUPPLY CLOSET

But the reason ethnography is built on participant observation is that it is about presence, "NOT BEHIND A SCREEN OF GLASS [but instead] RUBBING UP AGAINST CHILDREN, ABLE TO HEAR WHAT IS BEING SAID..."

...INTERACTING AND SHARING, TO SOME EXTENT, IN THEIR EXPERIENCES."
(GRAUE & WALSH p.107)

Even if the process is messy.

The idea of "headnotes" Graue & Walsh refer to is important because while FIELDNOTES are difficult to take while participating, HEADNOTES are not.

So, like anything else in my repertoire, observation is a tool—but with implications.

RIGHT. These tools are choices you make for specific reasons.

I might do more detached observation to get "the lay of the land." I could also become more involved as I develop rapport.

As long as you reflect and plan, you will make good choices.

which reminds me...

Rule # TWO:

HAVE A PLAN

If you just go someplace and sit there and think random observation will be useful, YOU WRONG.

Even observation that LOOKS quite casual and impromptu is certainly carefully planned!

There are lots of things to consider, even before you begin. Most importantly, CONTEXT.

Rule ONE was "Don't pretend to be a child," and Rule TWO is "Plan"?

These seem OBVIOUS.

Sit down. You know nothing.

When you visit the research context, think about where one can
— SIT?
— WALK?
— STAND?
— TAKE NOTES?
— PLAY?

Graue & Walsh also encourage us to be planful in noting any schedule: Are there times when one cannot move or talk or play?

Also, remember that CONTEXTS reflect POWER DYNAMICS.

Schools are popular research contexts, for example.

A B C D E F G H I J
a b c d e f g h i j

Schools are places where children are expected to answer adult questions and be obedient to adults.

Researchers need to plan to work in adult-controlled spaces, and places where adult control is mediated.

Punch (2002) writes, "Adults should not assume that children necessarily prefer their own environment. They may actually prefer an adult researcher NOT invade their child space..."

"...the implications of the research setting need to be considered with particular care..."

... awareness and sensitivity in research with children." (p. 328)

This kind of PLANNING is also part of the work of orienting yourself as a LEARNER.

You are there to LEARN how to be a member of the group.

And children love to teach about what they KNOW.

Approach accordingly.

Can I come in?

OKAY! NOW I am ready to plan and to observe!

Let's talk strategy.

You should start with,

★ Your research question

★ Your stance and role.

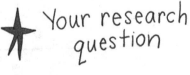

★ Your context

★ Your needs

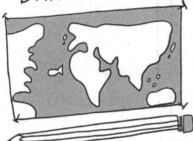

Then the NEXT thing you do is DRAW A MAP.

But I want to start OBSERVING!

NO.

Make a carefully drawn map, with labels, of your field site. It can be a simple drawing but should be something you can refer to later.

You will use it when you write about your site.

...elled like war... plastic, ... The cheerful brightly colored bins hel... eething rings in a rainbow of gelly colors, some ...ith soft toys hanging on bright rings just above t... padded, heavily sanitized changing table. Babies ...rooled onto their bibs and reached out with warm... ...ky hands to the ankles of standing adults who ...d do... ...licit so...ks and crie...

type
type
type

Writing about your site later is difficult without such careful documentation of context.

<u>Was</u> there a block area? I can't remember!

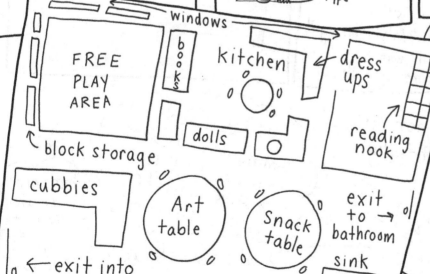

windows

FREE PLAY AREA

books

kitchen

dress ups

dolls

reading nook

block storage

cubbies

Art table

Snack table

exit to → bathroom

sink

← exit into hall

You can also show pathways and movement!

You can also annotate a panoramic photo, or use copies of your map in your field notes to periodically document the changing "lay of the land"

Maps can get even more detailed.

Mitchell & Reid-Walsh (2002) use them to READ a space.

Their analyses of children's popular culture involves looking at bedrooms.

"Reading" a child's bedroom tells us a lot about how children experience culture.

This goes well beyond labeling which furniture goes where.

Start by running your eyes over the space to "scan" for the dominant object or objects.

In their work, Mitchell & Reid-Walsh thought the crib was a dominant object.

At a school site, a dominant object might be the teacher's desk.

Now, MAP this object but not necessarily spatially. Think bigger!

Is the teacher who sits here also dominant?

Ask questions to guide observations!

if the desk feels dominant, what does that say about power in this context?

where are other related or opposite objects?

what do children do or not do around this object?

That is a very different kind of mapping! It's like the map is ALIVE!

This is a great way to take CUES from the context.

So, instead of mapping by drawing what you see, think about how it feels to be there, and implications thereof.

hey.

You can look at change by revisting your early maps.

What has changed?

Does it FEEL different?

TOYS

I've thought about role and stance and mapping and planning and NOW I AM READY TO OBSERVE!

... okay, but where do I LOOK?

WELCOME TO PRESCHOOL ♥ ♥ ♥ ♥

I thought I was ready.

some strategies will help.

Wolcott's (1981) work provides guidance.

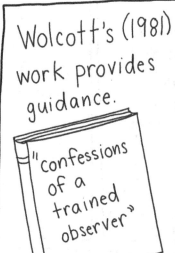

"confessions of a trained observer"

In this piece, Wolcott gives us FOUR STRATEGIES for getting started with observation.

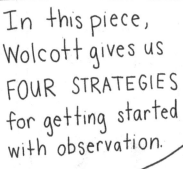

Admittedly, these may be more applicable on the non-participatory end of the observation continuum.

But they are still good for narrowing and focusing your observations.

And my research questions will also guide me.

correct.

Strategy number one:

OBSERVATION BY BROAD SWEEP

This is a good start because it helps you get a general sense of things AND it helps you become more selective as you go.

... But it is tricky too.

It's tricky to look at so much!

it's a lot to take in!

But you quickly find yourself drawn to what interests you.

What do you want to observe more closely?

As you do a BROAD SWEEP of the space...

Hmm. I keep gravitating back to the pretend play area...

The next strategy is the opposite of watching everything.

Strategy Number Two:

OBSERVATION OF NOTHING

How do you do THAT?

close your eyes?

Seriously, I jest. It is really more like zoning out to "wait and see."

WHAT JUMPS OUT!

BLAM!

...or what seems unusual, either to you or based on what you know about the context.

Victory!

TEACH

Like blips that pop up on a radar screen.

blip! blip! blip! blip!

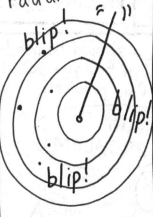

Trust me when I tell you that you will know what you are looking for when you see it.

The other two strategies kind of fit under the "look at nothing" umbrella.

Looking for things that are unusual!

Strategy #3:

OBSERVING FOR PARADOX

Delamont (2002) gives the example of a study that found children doing more drawing during their regular lessons than in their art lessons.

You might scan the context loosely with an eye on the things that don't fit.

The FOURTH strategy requires more of an emic perspective:

OBSERVING FOR PROBLEMS FACING THE GROUP

These might be clearly visible...

Ted STILL won't share!

... or they might require time to uncover.

ta-da!

You should be mindful of how you see and define problems.

LOUD PROBLEM!

QUIET PROBLEM

Searching for paradoxes and problems can also keep researchers alert—especially in contexts that may be overly familiar. (Delamont, 2002)

not seeing anything new...

Delamont (2002) adds a FIFTH strategy.

5

Pay attention to the things **PARTICIPANTS** are paying attention to!

Both explicitly...

Look at our classroom rules!

- SIT DOWN
- SHUT UP
- WORK HARD

and as a matter of course.

Stop looking out the window!

sigh...

Getting at the more subtle things means I would need a LOT of time at the field site...

to really SEE.

COOKIES

Try them all out! See what works!

FOCUSING

Your observations will focus over time.

all these strategies will help narrow your focus.

I cannot sustain strategy #one forever - but it will help me narrow my focus!

FOCUSING IS GREAT!

Focusing down is ultimately part of your research question — but also what you are seeing and learning as you observe.

At the end of the day

HOW

you look at things is more important than what you look at.

Delamont (2002) says it best:

"In an important sense it does not matter what the observer looks at, as long as the gaze is focused in a thoughtful, principled way ... [that] was reflexive, properly documented, and with a clear aim" (p. 132)

SO LOOK WELL, THINK DEEP, REFLECT OFTEN!

got it!

RULE NUMBER FOUR

DEVELOP YOUR STAMINA

Not really that kind of stamina.

WHAT?

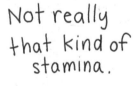

THIS KIND.

world's tiniest chair.

Hours of notes

One needs stamina to be able to spend enough time in the field doing the work of participant observation.

Participant observation should be of sufficient duration to support any claims you might make.

So you need to put in the time.

Hmm... what I saw in one hour is interesting — but is that happening <u>all</u> the time?

How long is long enough? How <u>much</u>?

An unusual event is informative in its own way — but it is not typical and should be noted as such.

This work is worth your time!

I am worth careful observation!

... so get ready to spend that time! But know that staying alert and watching for long periods of time is hard.

stamina.

Paying attention to your own process of participant observation can add layers of fatigue, potentially.

HEADSPACE

getting full...

And reflection can also be demanding.

I need to be disciplined, but also pace myself.

Physical note-taking can be exhausting.

ow!

It gets easier over time, but you might want to read up on others' ways of developing skills and *stamina*

You can extend this clarity by planning how you will communicate about what you are doing AND who you are as an observer.

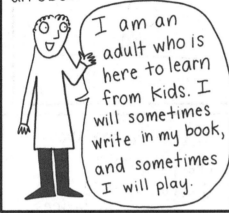

I am an adult who is here to learn from kids. I will sometimes write in my book, and sometimes I will play.

If you want to be ignored, keep a low profile and be consistent about it.

Oh him? He sits there. Let's go play.

If you want to be more participatory, James writes, "adopt a more fluid and conventional participatory approach" (252) Be flexible!

For example, Bluebond-Langner (1978) was very much a participant observer:

"Like a volunteer, and like most anthropologists in the field, I willingly did whatever they [the hospital staff] told me. I played with the children, helped with the meals, accompanied the children to various parts of the hospital and assisted in procedures" (p. 251)

This is a far cry from detached note-taking, with certainly different research questions and resulting data.

Participant observation can be very deep involvement.

"Although I was different things to different children, I was definitely part of their world of dying children. Of all the nonfamily persons, I was the only one who was always there, in a variety of situations, places and roles" (p. 247)

Bluebond-Langner's deep participatory involvement is part of what makes her work so powerful.

When doing observation, especially participant observation, keep FLUIDITY & FLEXIBILITY as your watchwords!

Bluebond-Langner's book is really moving.

Yes. It reminds me of the importance of descriptive research in childhood.

... and of our responsibility first and foremost to the child participant.

Can we talk about something VERY PRACTICAL now?

Sure.

We already talked about PLANNING— planning how to record observations...

HEADSPACE

OW

And we talked about the potential distractions of shiny, fancy, devices...

click click click

... and we championed a pen-and-paper approach while developing "headspace" and stamina.

But I want to know about the kinds of things researchers write down. What is the difference between "good" and "bad" fieldnotes?

Description vs. Interpretation!

Descriptions will be useful as data later on. Interpretations, not so much.

DESCRIPTION

"Tommy stomped his feet and furrowed his brow before knocking the blocks down."

INTERPRETATION

"Tommy was angry."

you can really sink your analytic teeth into a description

if you want or need to do BOTH, you should keep them separate using a DOUBLE-ENTRY note-taking system.

Describe	Interpret
Tommy stomps his feet and furrows his brow, knocking down the blocks.	Tommy is angry? Maybe note teacher response?

This column is where you interpret and jot down other ideas and questions, or memos for later.

... try to SHOW rather than simply TELLING.

Describe how things look, feel, smell and sound.

AND, transcribe your notes RIGHT AWAY!

Yes - I type mine up as soon as I can - every time!

But what if I have notes and also video—can I wait to transcribe it under those circumstances?

NO

Video can do lots of things— But it isn't the same as being there. You need to have a clear and planful reason to be using video. It's not just "backup."

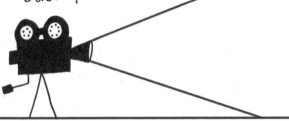

"Watching video can give the viewer a false sense of experiencing what she is viewing – of actually being there."

(Graue & Walsh p110)

You need to transcribe data RIGHT AWAY whether it's fieldnotes or video!

"It is not possible to record too much about a person, place, or interaction, but it is idiotic to pile up lots of material without reviewing it and beginning to reflect upon it.
Ten minutes of good observations, well-written up, is worth an hour's notes lying forgotten in an unopened notebook."

(Delamont, 2002, p. 138)

And there is a lot more to it than just watching

And that is just the beginning!

But in all this general talk about observation, we have forgotten a big idea...

NOT ALL CHILDREN ARE ALIKE!

I've been reading Sandstrom & Fine's <u>Knowing Children</u> (1988)

They remind us right off the bat that observating kids will look different at different ages.

All researchers in childhood have areas of specialization, but even some little knowledge about CHILD DEVELOPMENT helps us tailor our methods.

AH! And so we come FULL CIRCLE!

I'm not one to give too much space to developmentalism BUT I need some basic familiarity to help me understand kids a bit better.

I love what Sandstrom & Fine write about observers and preschoolers — that we are trying to understand them while they try to understand us!

This reminds me of how the researcher role is different when observing children.

It's about being an open-minded learner, while also being responsible and attuned to power differences.

Whew! Let's get to the HOMEWORK.

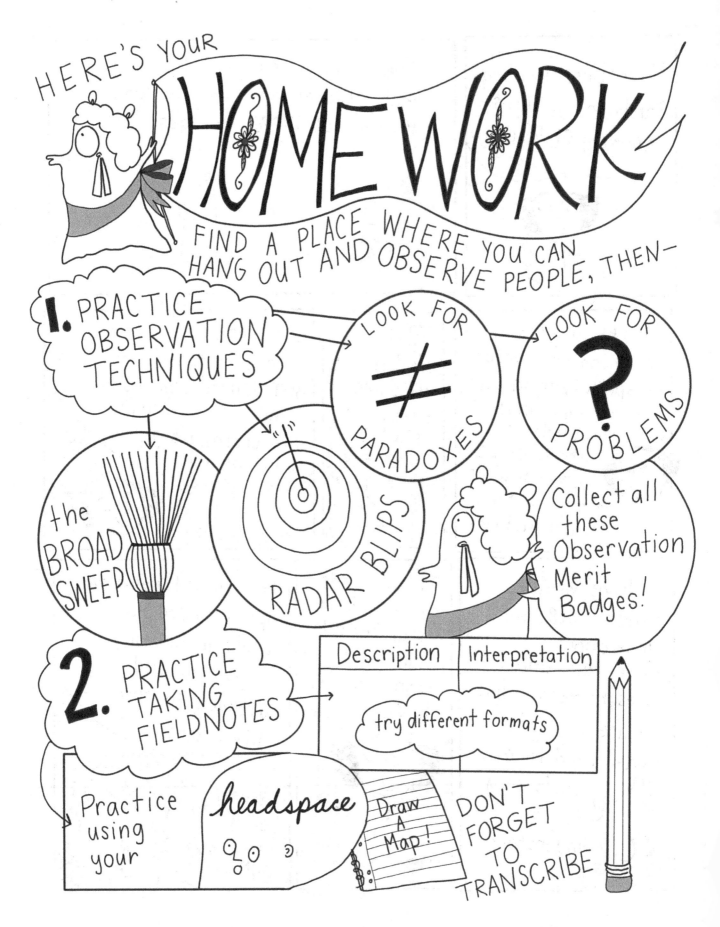

Chapter Seven

YES THAT LOOKS EXACTLY LIKE A GIRAFFE

Analyzing Children's Visual Products

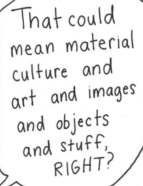

"Products" does not sound very, uh, **appetizing.**

Think of them as PICTURES or IMAGES that can be used to understand what kids know.

... And here to help you understand this tricky subject is Becky Anne's preschool self-portrait.

Hey there!

I can't decide if this is worse or better than the hamster.

I know a LITTLE bit about visual methods, like drawing...

... or collage,

... or painting, and photography.

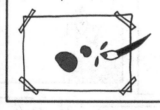

...and even making videos.

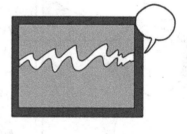

All those are awesome visual products!

Collecting material is one thing - but we are going to talk about how to analyze it.

And also how to involve child participants in analysis!

And... because you ARE an actual child's drawing...

yes!

Becky Anne drew me in preschool, but I've learned a lot since then.

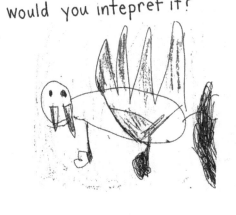

for example – take a look at this drawing. How would you interpret it?

Wow – I would say that is a scary monster.

NOW look what happens when we ask the **child** to interpret!

This is a picture of my best friend!

Your interpretation is still important. You might note your reactions and use them to structure the questions you ask children, or your own analytic memos.

You can also compare these across other children's products.

But please do continue to privilege the child's interpretation.

I LOVE MY FRIEND.

Seems simple! Got it. Let's move on.

Whoa! Not so fast! There is a LOT more to this. Let's start with a BIG QUESTION!

Why should we include visual products as data when we could just ASK kids to tell us what we want to know?

Okay, not so simple.

Don't gloat.

Weber & Mitchell (1995) write: "Drawings offer a different kind of glimpse into human sense-making than written or spoken texts do, because they can express that which is not easily put into words: the ineffable, the elusive, the not-yet-thought-through." (p.34)

Drawings are different and valuable!

You WOULD think so!

It's not just me. Lots of scholars agree.

DRAWINGS as visual PRODUCTS make sense in many DIFFERENT WAYS!

Creative methods like drawing give children time to think.

WHAT NEXT?

... and enable them to build ideas gradually rather than forcing an immediate response (Gauntlett, 2004)

Creative methods also give children time to accommodate for having less practiced and developed comprehension skills (Harden et al, 2000)

We also know these skills also vary person by person. (Hill, 2006)

... and language and literacy skills do not always match cognitive skills. (Horstman et al, 2008)

And adults don't always understand what kids are talking about without help. (Punch, 2002)

Using drawings can address all these issues!

Sign me up!

Wait just a minute - While I don't deny the benefits, we need to THINK deeply and carefully before we go too crazy.

We should not always assume that ALL children will enjoy drawing and be able and comfortable expressing themselves in this way.

Not all children feel good about art as a means of expression.

I would rather just talk about how I feel.

Also, there are loads of potential analytic pitfalls associated with adult interpretation.

All the children drew giraffes because they like spots.

(Many of the analytic issues can be addressed if researchers are a bit more CLEAR in describing processes and issues.

Then there's the **Cute Problem**: People add drawings or other visual data because it seems **cute** and **fun**.

throw in some art!

WOO HOO!

When it really should be for more principled reasons related to content, questions, or plan.

My picture was NOT of a giraffe.

The arts in research are NOT cute add-ons!

Okay - I will be thoughtful, reflective, and purposeful about THIS too...

Now let's talk VISUAL PRODUCTS!

The heaviest hitter in the game is the beautifully and simply named,

Draw and Write technique

For real, a participant draws and writes. That is it!

It came out of research in public health in the early 1970's

Timmy won't talk but maybe he will DRAW about his lung flukes.

Pioneered by Wetton, it was recast by Angell et al (2011) as

Draw and Write and TELL!

The "TELL" part is the new bit, bringing in the interpretation of the artist.

my picture is...

At its most basic, DRAW & WRITE meant asking a child to draw a picture in response to a question and then write down any ideas.

kids draw here.

kids write here.

With the addition of TELL we learn so much more.

On one hand it was nice to have both drawing and writing to analyze.

the ocean fishes?

And on the other hand, having kids TELL as well resulted in good conversations.

I drew a SHARK because I like TEETH.

Kids could refer back to drawings — and older and younger kids could participate at their own levels.

I don't remember so I will look at my picture.

Drawing AND writing generated better ideas than just writing alone (Pridmore & Lansdown, 1997)

Oh yeah, I like fishes too.

It is flexible, and as long as researchers are consistent.

I need to record how I ask each question.

It is also very good at getting shy or younger children to express themselves.

shark.

Bradding & Horstman (1999) think that drawing methods might even be more ethical, because children might have more control over the disclosure of information.

I draw what I want.

Children feel in-charge. This might mediate any power dynamics.

I feel like this is almost _so_ child-friendly that it is hard for there to be too many problems.

The really key part is in the ALMOST!

The "tell" part is how we can at least partially guard against "Adult attempts to place their own interpretation on the words and drawings of children."

(Backett-Milburn & Mckie, 1999, p 397)

Another thing to SERIOUSLY watch out for is the phrase, "CHILD FRIENDLY"

STOP

It isn't always grounded in our understanding of the child and context, but instead in the assumption that anything an adult thinks will appeal to a child will actually _be_ appealing or attractive!

I loved playing with rocks when I was a kid, so lets base this project on playing with rocks! It's CHILD-FRIENDLY!

Like my clown suit idea.

YES.

I wonder what a child would consider "child-friendly"?

Probably not the same thing most adult researchers do.

"child-friendly is more complicated than it seems.

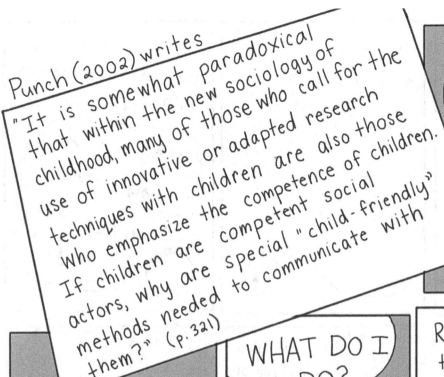

Punch (2002) writes

"It is somewhat paradoxical that within the new sociology of childhood, many of those who call for the use of innovative or adapted research techniques with children are also those who emphasize the competence of children. If children are competent social actors, why are special "child-friendly" methods needed to communicate with them?" (p. 321)

my clown suit was an even worse idea than I thought.

I just can't get it right.

WHAT DO I DO?

Relax. Let's go back to REFLECTION and RAPPORT!

Get to KNOW the children in your context — think about your process. Go from there!

It's really only the people adding what they think are cute "extras" that fall into this trap.

I'm an ADULT and I find lots of these methods to be friendlier than traditional methods. Punch (2002) calls all of these "task-based" methods. I like that.

Adults sometimes like task-based methods like drawing too!

We get to DRAW?

So we take "child-friendly" with a grain of salt.

salt

AND we ground our use of these methods with REFLECTION.

Why am I doing this? what does it do?

It is a balance.

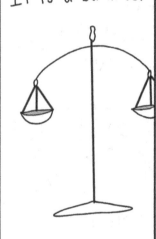

some critiques suggest that children only draw what they can easily represent.

Can you draw a picture of yourself?

I drew a horse because I am good at drawing horses.

Ah. A horse.

Maybe if we also provide stencils and collage materials and kids can choose what they like.

Great thinking! And if you provide collage materials, choose them carefully for leading or biased responses.

DIST TRE | RIDIC PEO | GIANT MAN | VAGUE SEXISM

(e.g. limit magazines)

Finally, it is worth repeating - not all kids like drawing.

I can't make my drawings look the way I want.

When representation becomes stressful for children, step BACK.

It doesn't look good!

Be sensitive and flexible. Provide options. Always have a plan B. And remember that children can stop being in the study at any time.

Would you like to use legos instead?

You might want to consider trying multiple tasks together to provide options for children who may be stressed by representation concerns.

Drawing isn't the ONLY way to create a visual product. You may wish to try photography!

selfie!

:CLICK:

Photographs can be taken with many devices some kids are already familiar with.

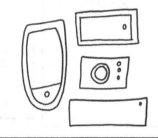

Also, photographing something may not require the same small motor skills or artistic accuracy, so some children may find it less daunting. (Punch, 2002)

I took a GREAT picture!

Children feel able to participate and make images that look how they want them to look.

no stress here

Of course there are ETHICAL considerations that apply to photography.

It's useful that kids can take cameras into places the researcher cannot really go...

But researchers should have a plan in place for what to do if a child takes a photograph that suggests an unsafe environment, for example.

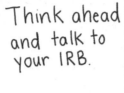

Think ahead and talk to your IRB.

ALWAYS PLAN AHEAD

Also, you should be sensitive to the socioeconomic dimensions potentially in play.

I can't afford one.

A child in your study might really love photography.

Finally I can express myself!

But owning a camera of their own may not be possible.

How will you address this accessibility issue? (Punch, 2002)

Why did I learn that anyway?

And that is really just the tip of the photo iceberg.

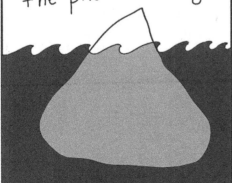

This is the part where I tell you to look in the back of the book for "further reading"

Good researchers read other researchers' work, after all!

NOW...
HOW DO WE DO
The *Analysis* PART?

Because that is super tricky and also important.

You may have collected tons of visual material,

But now wonder, how do I begin to INTERPRET?

You might have a conversation with a child about what they created.

I drew a horse.

Why?

You might have even been present during its creation
Now I make the tail...

Maybe you were able to ask questions along the way.
Why is the tail important?

You really have three "streams" of data. More data helps you interpret more clearly.
MORE DATA TO MANAGE?

1. The actual DRAWINGS (or other products)

2. Written ideas or notes
a horse.

3. spoken explanations (e.g. "tell")
I only know how to draw horses.

"To ensure that all the data are used and interpreted correctly, it is essential to **MARRY UP** the child's interpretation with the content of their drawing and text."

(Angell, Alexander & Hunt, 2011, p348)

This means keeping it **TOGETHER** – and analyzing the material as a unit, not as independent items.

Here we have organized folios primarily by participant.

You might also include your notes and any memos you write as part of each data folio.

Folios are holistic.

Can we get back to analysis, though? I hear you that we privilege the child's interpretation.

And I understand the part about holistic organizing. But it all still feels FUNNY.

Funny? How?

It feels like I am **PSYCHOANALYZING** the children's visual products — And that feels wrong!

I looked at some popular press books and they had titles like,

WHAT ARE the HIDDEN MEANINGS IN YOUR KID'S ART

YUCK!

Well, rest assured you are NOT in the business of "exposing" hidden meaning. No way.

You are about **INTERPRETATION & UNDERSTANDING**

In exposing-type analyses, the child participant is an uninvolved object. It is decontextualized and about individual sussing out rather than seeking emic understanding.

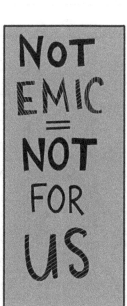

NOT EMIC = NOT FOR US

Remember, we operate from a core belief that children can participate and contribute...

AS KNOWERS & COMPETENT SOCIAL ACTORS.

That "psychoanalytic" feeling you describe may be a sign that, in your analyses, you might be superimposing your own ideas onto the data.

IDEAS

You have great ideas BUT...

We must "not impose inappropriate interpretations ...children's generational position tends to mean that an adult has access to wider knowledge to be more able to analyze children's social status."

(Punch, 2002, p. 327)

While we are wary of and critique the "child-friendly"...

...we make every effort to be CHILD-CENTERED.

This means putting them at the center,

NOT as objects of study BUT as RESPECTED KNOWERS

I feel a little better. I also feel like I learned an important lesson in listening to my feelings.

RIGHT. Always listen to that small itch that says something is not right.

So, I hear from children, ask clarifying questions about their meaning, and center their interpretation.

Is that it?

WAIT THERE'S MORE!

you can:

count how many and how often

do content analysis: what's there? what isn't there?

think about how children treat your prompt

see how drawings and other data change over time:

compare which participants drew what.

Of course it depends on your research question - but you can think creatively too!

As long as you stay reflective and listen to your feelings.

And remember to draw on what you know best as an ethnographer: CONTEXT.

meow

Children in this study drew their pets as friends – and gave them human qualities and special emotional abilities.

Researcher thinking

Maybe the researcher will have more questions, maybe not.

But can you see how VISUAL PRODUCTS are used? How it is centered on the child in context?

totally!

If you are centering the child's interpretation and you are familiar with the context, and you consistently reflect on your position and assumptions you can do some fantastic work with visual products.

What if I notice that something is missing? Something that I would expect to see?

Analysis of what is "not there" is also important!

If you really know the research context you will be more likely to notice what is noticeably absent, and formulate ideas about why...

Stokrocki & Samoraj (2002) analyzed art from Polish Catholic children about attending and experiencing Mass.

They noticed that the children drew objects but did not reference spiritual content.

That was pretty surprising!

What's NOT there is key.

And even though we are asking children to interpret their work...

love

... we are also analyzing children's products in the larger study context.

We must analyze the data we get from the Draw, Write and Tell approach, not just report it.

Let's try this prompt: "Draw a picture of an animal"

this is my cat I love heR. Anb sizteR.

Chloe, age 5.

There are many things here to explore.

♥ You might ask the child more about why she loves her cat.

♥ You could consider why her sister is smaller than the cat, and also why the sister is even in the picture.

♥ You could count the kinds of animals all the children in the study drew – did they draw pets? Real or pretend animals?

♥ Think about the context. Is this in a rural setting where children might have more and different experiences with animals?

CHAPTER SEVEN ♥Homework♥

1. Come up with a short two or three question "interview" you might conduct with a child.

2. Now devise a visual-generating prompt on the same topic.

3. Try both ways of getting information from a child you know.

4. Be sure to have the child write and/or tell about the picture.

5. What was different? What was the same?

Chapter Eight

Research Ethics

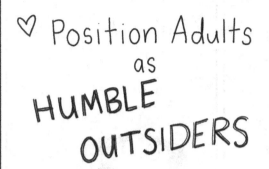

♡ Position Adults as HUMBLE OUTSIDERS

First we position children as the decision-makers and now we consider how to think still differently, about the adult researcher.

So, even though you _were_ a child,

It is not a country you know any longer.

Being an outsider changes the ethical field, and demands that you actively interrogate any slips into "insider" assumptions.

AN OUTSIDER in ethnographic work is very different from AN INSIDER, and has different perspectives.

OUTSIDERS
→ are allowed to be less participatory & should orient themselves as learners
→ are humble permission-seekers.
→ sometimes fail to really "get" what is going on.

INSIDERS
→ members of the group who must navigate insider status while working as a researcher.
→ may take for granted what they see.*
→ fall victim to errors of "over-rapport" (Hammersley & Atkinson 1995)

"the ethnographer needs to be intellectually poised between familiarity and strangeness." (Brayboy & Deyhle, 2000, p.163)

*this is still a risk for adult researchers who were once children.

And finally, be wary of *The cult of cute*

But kids ARE cute!

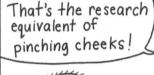

That's the research equivalent of pinching cheeks!

...and a red flag! As a regular person you can cute-it-up all you like, but...

But as a researcher it spells disaster.

If all you see is how cute I am you will miss the rest, and judge me when I am not cute.

This reminds me of when we talked earlier about how sometimes white middle class researchers only see white middle class children as cute while they adultify children of color...

gasp What is wrong with that child?!?

I'M A KILLER BEE!

If all you expect is a golden cherub you will not treat children ethically ... and you really will do poor work.

So, when we talked about kids being full and complete people, that means getting past one-dimensional "cute".

So, get past it. Be thoughtful, be careful, be good and fair in thinking about participants!

Okay- I need to be a humble learner who treats kids as full people and puts them in charge. I'm so sleepy...

That's a good start, but refill your coffee and prepare to listen.

Friends at home might want to review IRB basics before reading on.

All that other stuff was the INSIDE YOUR HEAD type preparation. But now we need to go over some OUTSIDE YOUR HEAD rules and regs and other stuff!

I ♥ Paperwork

Yes, this is the part with all the paperwork.

so go get yourself a hat,

and hold onto it.

When we think about research with children in the ethnographic tradition, the type of IRB permission we want is called

SOCIAL-BEHAVIORAL

(the other stuff falls under "medical-biological" and it is another thing altogether.)

IRB approval rests on

♥ Benefit vs. Risk
♥ Protections
♥ Permissions

with regard to

BENEFITS & RISKS

they must be balanced.

♡ Who can give permission? Who can assent?

♡ How can you guard against coercion?

♡ How can you recognize when a child doesn't assent?

♡ What happens if you suspect abuse or neglect?

Can we review a little?

Okay—back to basics we go!

The history of child protection in most of the world is not good.

COAL MINE

Children get special protections in many places but that does not mean that all is hunky dory.

abuse/neglect, trafficking, child labor, etc. all the time, everywhere.

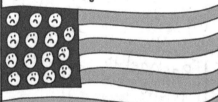

The U.S. has refused to ratify the UN Convention on the Rights of the Child.

Ostensibly so far right parents can continue to beat and miseducate them.

This all means that as researchers we must be doubly attentive, and carefully regulate our work.

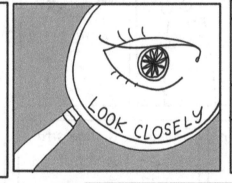

LOOK CLOSELY

some people think it's too much regulation!

Tell me, fellow adult, how do you think kids feel?

Maybe even creating LESS research with children.

To get at child research issues more indepth, we will use the United States as a case, but recognize that things can vary.

♥ 18 is the age of majority.

♥ under 18 can assent but not consent.

Wards can only be included if the research is About being a ward,

or it is conducted in a setting where the majority are NOT wards,

And the IRB will require that Mason have a special advocate.

Historically, wards went unprotected.

bad researcher

defenseless wards

It was basically open season.

But what about Rachael?

Rachael isn't exactly a child, either.

She is an Emancipated Minor

This means that she is treated as an adult even though she is under 18.

Maybe she is self supporting and not living with parents.

maybe she is married,*

Or pregnant or a parent.

Or in the military.

or declared to be emancipated by the courts for a different reason.

just cuz.

* Ew. But still.

Meanwhile...

Research that is "Sorta Bad"

2

has some risks but the research is still beneficial.

This kind involves greater-than-minimal risk...

bigger than normal bear ↓

But still has the prospect of direct benefit to the individual child study participant.

Direct benefit:

We learned so much by piloting our new therapy with traumatized Timmy.

I feel better!

Timmy is likely to BENEFIT from the therapy study even if talking about trauma is RISKY.

This is NOT a direct benefit:

We made Timmy relive his trauma to design treatment to help others.

And even with direct benefit you must still be scrupulous about assent and permission.

ASSENT   PERMISSION

NOW...

Research at level 3 is Kinda Bad and not so much beneficial...

3

Here we have greater than minimal risk but without any direct benefit.

So, no direct benefit to the individual child participant.

BUT the research may offer a benefit in the form of general knowledge.

Others might benefit.

Consider some kinds of medical research where an intervention might exceed minimal risk.

↑ giant needle

Or consider education research on a specific rare learning disability

Pulled out of class and subjected to a lot of arduous tests.

So, above minimal risk...

maybe also video recorded to document frustration and fatigue

... but the study is unlikely to yield ways to help participant children with the condition.

The study procedures are not dangerous but also not pleasant, but will be worth valuable eventual findings.

future child benefits!

Lastly...

Research at our level FOUR is really quite bad and not at all beneficial.

How is this worth it?

You might find this in biomedical research when a child has a very rare condition with few chances for study or a cure.

A study involving this level of risk may require a higher level of research permission such as a 407 or HHS Review.

Now do you begin to see, Cherie?

And I am getting very HUNGRY.

WAIT! WAIT! I still don't understand! What is the difference between consent and assent?

Okay.

Unless you have been living under a rock you have probably seen a consent form.

consent form
This study is about my research and I really need you to participate if at all possible The risks and benefits are all pretty uninteresting but I'm going to go through it all in detail just in case the IRB really does read all of this. I am quite cert they'd

For CHILDREN to participate in research they cannot give CONSENT but instead they

ASSENT

to participation and their parents/guardians give PERMISSION.

If you have, in fact, been living under a rock, please visit the "HOMEWORK" section at the end of this chapter.

ASSENT means A child's affirmative agreement to participate.

♡. The child must show willingness.

♡ The child must do more than simply obey.

♡ The child must understand.

Not every child can assent.

(for some, the IRB might waive assent)

(small baby)

And, assent must be AFFIRMATIVE. Failure to object is not the same as assent.

asleep... or assenting?

baddie

The language of assent must be age-appropriate.

Assent blah blah blah blah blah blah blah blah blah ? ?

For adolescents, whose capacities may be closer to adults', assent can be much more like a consent document.

Young children need assent in simple language to help them really understand.

NO.

Hi! My name is Tim and I am a researcher. I am trying to learn about ____. I want to ask if you will help me. First I want to explain what you would be doing if you do decide you want to help. Okay?

Okay! Tell me about it.

Parents and guardians give permission for a child to participate.

Even if the parent says yes, anything other than a strong yes from the child is a NO.

YES

um...

Likewise, if the parent says NO it is a NO.

NO.

And without a parental YES you do not even ask the child.

Classroom research is often a special case.

You will need to get permission and assent for all involved students.

I lost my paper.

Or you might have to change design.

Yes   Yes   Yes   Yes   Yes   ?   Yes   Yes   Yes

Sometimes "my backpack ate my permission letter."

You may consider providing a small incentive like a pencil or a sticker to each child when they return their permission form, whether or not their parent gives permission.

or do the parent permission in person at a school event. You can also answer any questions.

all set!

You need a plan for what to do if you suspect abuse or neglect.

Always check in with the nice folks at the IRB for guidance!

Also, you should find out if you are a **mandatory reporter.**

uh...

You might be a mandatory reporter if you are any of these people:

A DOCTOR   A NURSE   A TEACHER   A POLICE OFFICER

Podiatrist	Day Care Worker	Foster Parent ♡
Bus Driver	School Counselor	Art therapist
Lawyer	Dentist	The list goes on and on.

In most places mandatory reporters MUST report suspected child abuse or neglect.

In many places, they are also protected from any legal problems that might result from making a report.

And in most places there are legal penalties for failing to make a report when you had reasonable suspicion.

See why you need to know?

Yep.

This awareness even shows up in assent and permission documents.

It has ramifications for confidentiality!

Yes!

ASSENT DOCUMENT

We will not tell anyone what you tell us unless there is something you tell us that could be dangerous to you or someone else. If you tell us that someone has been hurting you we may have to tell people who can help keep you safe.

PARENT PERMISSION

Under the law the researcher cannot maintain as confidential any information about known or reasonably suspected child abuse or neglect. If any researcher is given such information they may be required to tell the police.

And the language will vary by location and your reporter status.

Right. Check with your IRB.

We want children to be safe, and you too!

Speaking of being safe, what is this rash?

That is a whole different kind of safety.

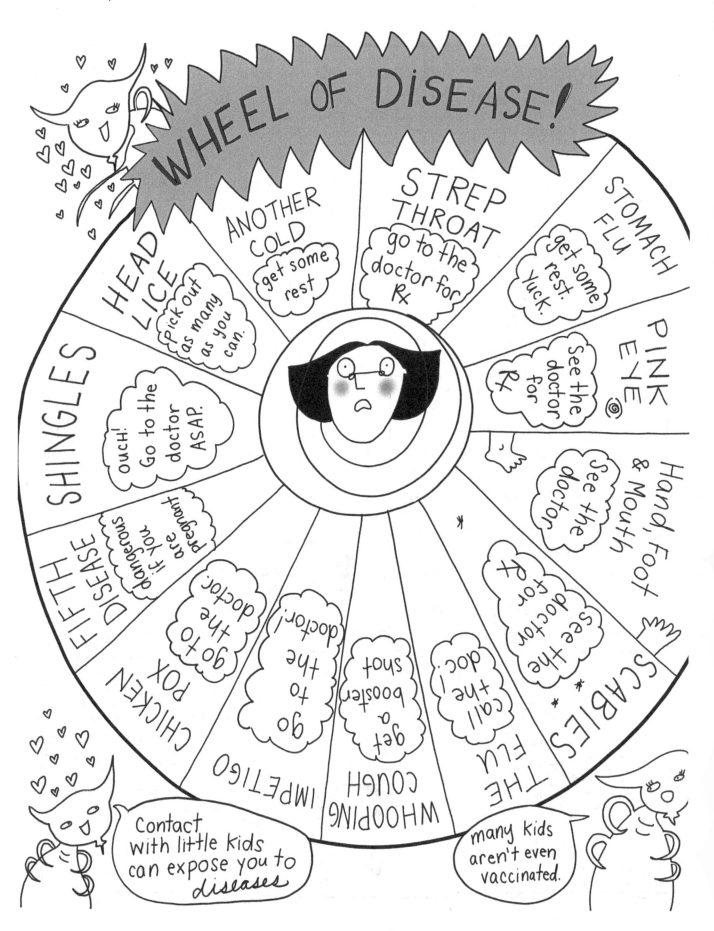

Homework

♥. Get familiar with your local IRB and find out what you need to know about research with children. Obtain copies of assent and permission templates.

♥ Talk to someone who does research with children. What practical advice can they offer? Ask ALL your questions!

Chapter Nine

★ THE BALLAD OF LITTLE SHANE ☆

CONCLUDING THOUGHTS

"Therefore, I would argue that it is too simplistic to consider research with children as one of two extremes: either the same or different from adults. Instead it should be seen as on a continuum where the way that research with children is perceived moves back and forth along the continuum according to a variety of factors: individual children, the questions asked, the research context, whether they are younger or older children and the researcher's own attitudes and behavior. Researchers need to be reflexive throughout the research process and critically aware of the range of reasons why research with children may be potentially different from research with adults. Perceiving children as competent social actors does not necessarily mean that research should be conducted in the same way as with adults. This is because many of the reasons underlying potential differences stem from children's marginalized position in adult society or from our own adult perceptions of children rather than being a reflection of children's competencies" (Punch, 2002, p. 338).

While Shane is reading up on all things Ethnography of Childhood, you should get started as well. So, for your final HOMEWORK assignment, you are going to do some reading!

HOMEWORK # 9

Go back through all your homework for the other chapters.

Do a quick jot-down analysis of the important ideas in each one and record them here.

Also make notes of what you READ in each homework. Start a list of your favorites! Keep growing it!

Make copies of any drawings and make notes about what each means.

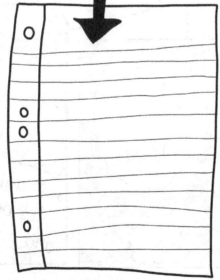

Attach these materials together either physically or in a computer file.

I prefer the tactile way!

also include any tools you developed or other ideas you had.

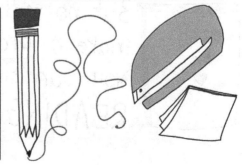

The End!

Happy Researching!

love,
Shane

further reading

Barker, J. & Weller, S. (2003). "Is it fun?" developing children centred research methods. *International Journal of Sociology and Social Policy*, 23 (1–2), 33–58.

Behar, R. (1996). *The vulnerable observer: Anthropology that breaks your heart.* Beacon Press: Boston.

Best, J. (1994). *Troubling children: Studies of children and social problems.* Piscataway: Transaction Publishers.

Bellino, M. J. (2017). *Youth in postwar Guatemala: Education and civic identity in transition.* New Brunswick, NJ: Rutgers University Press.

Bettelheim, B. (1976). *The uses of enchantment: The meaning and importance of fairy tales.* New York: Vintage Books.

Brumberg, J. J. (1998). *The body project: An intimate history of American girls.* New York: Vintage Books.

Calvert, K. (1992). *Children in the house: The material culture of early childhood, 1600–1900.* Boston: Northeastern University Press.

Cheney, K. (2007). *Pillars of the nation: Child citizens and Ugandan national development.* Chicago: University of Chicago Press.

Christakis, E. (2016). *The importance of being little: What preschoolers really need from grownups.* New York, New York: Viking.

Coles, R. (1986). *The moral life of children.* New York: Atlantic Monthly Press.

Coles, R. (1989). *The call of stories: Teaching and the moral imagination.* Boston: Houghton Mifflin.

Coontz, S. (2016). *The way we never were: American families and the nostalgia trap.* New York: Basic Books.

Corsaro, W. A. (2004). *We're friends, right?: Inside kids' culture.* Washington, D.C: Joseph Henry Press.

D'Amato, J. (1988). "Acting": Hawaiian children's resistance to teachers. *The Elementary School Journal*, 88(5), 529–544.

Davies, B. (2003). *Frogs and snails and feminist tales: Preschool children and gender.* Cresskill, NJ: Hampton Press.

Dyson, A. H. (1997). *Writing superheroes: Contemporary childhood, popular culture and contemporary literacy.* New York: Teachers College Press.

Edelman, M. R. (1992). *The measure of our success: A letter to my children and yours.* Boston: Beacon.

Egan, K. (1999). *Children's minds, talking rabbits and clockwork oranges: Essays on education.* New York: Teachers College Press.

Ehrensaft, D. & Spack, N. (2016). *The gender creative child: Pathways for nurturing and supporting children who live outside gender boxes.* New York: The Experiment.

Fader, A. (2018). *Mitzvah girls.* Princeton, NJ: Princeton University Press.

Fadiman, A. (1997). *The spirit catches you and you fall down: A Hmong child, her American doctors, and the collision of two cultures.* New York: Farrar, Strauss and Giroux.

Fass, P., & Mason, M. (Eds.). (2000). *Childhood in America.* New York: NYU Press.

Galman, S. (2013). *The good, the bad and the data: A beginner's guide to qualitative data analysis.* London: Routledge.

Galman, S. C. (2015). Mischief-making of one kind/and another: Unruliness and resistance in rural preschoolers' play. *Ethnography and Education 10* (3), 310–324.

Galman, S. C. (2018). The story of Peter Both-in-One: Using visual storytelling methods to understand risk and resilience among transgender and gender-nonconforming young children in rural North American contexts. In A. Mandrona & C. Mitchell (Eds.), *Visual encounters in the study of rural childhoods.* Camden, NJ: Rutgers University Press.

Galman, S. C. & Mallozzi, C. A. (2015). There are no girl pirate captains: Boys, girls and the "boy crisis" in preschool. *Boyhood Studies, 8* (1), 33–46.

Geertz, C. (1973). *The interpretation of cultures: Selected essays.* New York: Basic Books.

Grace, D.J. & Lum A. L. P. (2001). "We don't want no haole buttholes in our stories": Local girls reading the Baby-Sitters Club books in Hawai'i. *Curriculum Inquiry* 31 (4): 451–452.

Hains, R. C. (2014). *The princess problem: Guiding our girls through the princess-obsessed years.* Naperville, Illinois: Sourcebooks.

Heath, S. B. (1983). *Ways with words: Life and work in communities and classrooms.* Cambridge University Press.

Henward, A. S. (2015). "She don't know I got it. You ain't gonna tell her, are you?" Popular culture as resistance in American preschools. *Anthropology & Education Quarterly, 46*(3), 208–223.

hooks, b. (1997). *Bone black: Memories of girlhood.* New York: Holt.

Jenkins, H. (Ed.) (1998). *The children's culture reader.* New York: NYU Press.

Lancy, D. F. (2015). *The anthropology of childhood: Cherubs, chattel, changelings.* Cambridge: Cambridge University Press.

Leavitt, R. L. (1994). *Power and emotion in infant-toddler day care.* Albany: SUNY Press.

Lukose, R. A. (2009). *Liberalization's children: Gender, youth, and consumer citizenship in globalizing India.* Durham NC: Duke University Press Books.

Malone, K. (2017). *Children in the Anthropocene: Rethinking sustainability and child friendliness in cities.* New York: Palgrave Macmillan.

Margulis, J. (Ed.) (2003). *Toddler: Real life stories of those fickle, irrational, urgent, tiny people we love.* New York: Seal Press.

Markstrom, A. & Hallden, G. (2009). Children's strategies for agency in preschool. *Children and Society, 23,* 112–122.

Mazzarella, S. R., & Pecora, N. O. (Eds.) (2002). *Growing up girls: Popular culture and the construction of identity.* New York: Peter Lang.

Melton, G. B., Ben-arieh, A., Cashmore, J., Goodman, G. S., & Worley, N. K. (Eds.) (2013). *The SAGE handbook of child research.* London: SAGE Publications Ltd.

Mendoza-Denton, N. (2008). *Homegirls: Language and cultural practice among Latina youth gangs.* Malden, MA: Wiley-Blackwell.

Mintz, S. (2006). *Huck's raft_: A history of American childhood.* Boston: Harvard University Press.

Miller, A. (1981). *The drama of the gifted child.* New York: Basic Books.

Morris, M., Conteh, M., & Harris-Perry, M. (2018). *Pushout: The criminalization of Black girls in schools* (First Trade Paper edition). The New Press.

Orenstein, P. (1994). *Schoolgirls: Young women, self-esteem and the confidence gap.* New York, NY: Doubleday.

Paley, V. G. (1987). *Wally's stories.* Boston: Harvard University Press.

Paley, V. G. (2004). *A child's work: The importance of fantasy play.* Chicago: University of Chicago Press.

Parnell, W., & Iorio, J. M. (Eds.). (2016). *Disrupting early childhood education research: Imagining new possibilities.* New York: Routledge.

Polakow, V. (1992). *The erosion of childhood.* Chicago: University of Chicago Press.

Qvortrup, J. (1994). *Childhood matters.* Aldershot, UK: Avebury.

Renold, E., & Allan, A. (2006). Bright and beautiful: High achieving girls, ambivalent femininities, and the feminization of success in the primary school. *Discourse: Studies in the Cultural Politics of Education, 27*(4), 457–473.

Rogoff, B. (1990). *Apprenticeship in thinking: Cognitive development in social context.* Oxford: Oxford University Press.

Roland-Martin, J. (1992). *The schoolhome: Rethinking schools for changing families.* Boston: Harvard University Press.

Rose, M. (1995). *Possible lives: The promise of public education in America.* New York:Penguin Books.

Scheper-Hughes, N., & Sargent, C. F. (Eds.) (1999). *Small wars: The cultural politics of dhildhood.* Berkeley: University of California Press.

Solomon, A. (2013). *Far from the tree: Parents, children and the search for identity.* New York: Scribner.

Spradley, J. P. (1980). *Participant observation.* New York: Holt, Rinehart and Winston.

Spitz, E. H. (1999). *Inside picture books.* New Haven: Yale University Press.

Stack, C. (1970). *All our kin.* New York: Basic Books.

Strauss, A., & Corbin, J. M. (1998). *Basics of qualitative research: Techniques and procedures for developing grounded theory.* Thousand Oaks, CA: SAGE Publications.

Stephens, S. (1995). *Children and the politics of culture.* Princeton, NJ: Princeton University Press.

Tobin, J., Hsueh, Y., & Karasawa, M. (2011). *Preschool in three cultures revisited: China, Japan, and the United States.* Chicago: University of Chicago Press.

Tobin, J., Arzubiaga, A., & Adair, J. K. (2013). *Children crossing borders: Immigrant parent and teacher perspectives on preschool for children of immigrants.* New York: Russell Sage Foundation.

Van Maanen, J. (2011). *Tales of the field: On writing ethnography.* Chicago: University Of Chicago Press.

Willis, P. (1981). *Learning to labor: How working class kids get working class jobs.* New York: Columbia University Press.

Wohlwend, K. E. (2004). Chasing friendship. *Childhood Education, 81*(2), 77–82.

Wohlwend, K. E. (2012). "Are you guys girls?": Boys, identity texts, and Disney princess play. *Journal of Early Childhood Literacy, 12*(1), 3–23.

Wu, B. (2011). *Whose culture has capital? Class, culture, migration and mothering.* Bern: Peter Lang.

Bibliography

Ainsworth, M. D. S. (1973). The development of infant-mother attachment. In B. Cardwell & H. Ricciuti (Eds.), *Review of child development research* (Vol. 3, pp. 1–94). Chicago: University of Chicago Press.

Angell, C., Alexander, J., & Hunt, J. A. (2015). Draw, write and tell: A literature review and methodological development on the 'draw and write' research method. *Journal of Early Childhood Research* 13 (1): 17–28.

Angell, C., Alexander, J., & Hunt, J. A. (2011). How are babies fed? A pilot study exploring primary school children's perceptions of infant feeding. *Birth* 38 (4): 346–53.

Angulo-Barroso, R. M., Schapiro, L., Liang, W., Rodrigues, O., Shafir, T., Kaciroti, N., Jacobson, S. W., & Lozoff, B. (2011). Motor development in 9-month-old infants in relation to cultural differences and iron status. *Developmental Psychobiology* 53 (2): 196–210. Aries, P. (1962). *Centuries of childhood.* New York: Vintage.

Backett-Milburn, K. & McKie, L. (1999). A critical appraisal of the draw and write technique. *Health Education Research* 14, 387–398.

Balagopalan, S. (2014). *Inhabiting 'childhood': Children, labour and schooling in postcolonial India.* London: Palgrave MacMillan.

Benedict, R. (1934). *Patterns of culture.* New York: Harcourt Brace.

Benedict, R. (1955). Continuities and discontinuities in cultural conditioning. In M. Mead and M. Wolfenstein (Eds.), *Childhood in contemporary cultures*, pp. 21–30. Chicago: University of Chicago Press.

Bluebond-Langner, M. (1980). *The private worlds of dying children.* Princeton, NJ: Princeton University Press.

Boas, F. (1974). Human faculty as determined by race. In G.W. Stocking (Ed.), *The shaping of American anthropology, 1883–1911: A Franz Boas Reader*, pp. 221–242. New York: Basic Books (originally published 1894).

Bowlby, J. (1958). The nature of the child's tie to his mother. *International Journal of Psychoanalysis, 39,* 350–371.

Bowlby J. (1969). *Attachment.* New York: Basic Books.

Bradding, A., & Horstman, M. (1999). Using the write and draw technique with children. *European Journal of Oncology Nursing, 3*(3), 3170–175.

Brayboy, & Deyhle, D. (2000). Insider-outsider: Researchers in American Indian communities. *Theory into Practice*, 39(3), 163–169.

Bronfenbrenner, U. (1979). *The ecology of human development: Experiments by nature and design.* Cambridge, MA: Harvard University Press.

Canella, G. S. (1997). *Deconstructing early childhood education.* New York: Peter Lang.

Chapin, B. L. (2014). *Childhood in a Sri Lankan village: Shaping hierarchy and desire.* New Brunswick: Rutgers University Press.

Delamont, S. (2002). *Fieldwork in educational settings: Methods, pitfalls and perspectives* (2nd Ed.). New York: Routledge.

Ferguson, A. A. (2001). *Bad boys: Public schools and the making of Black masculinity.* Ann Arbor MI: University of Michigan Press.

Fine, G. A. & Sandstrom, K. L. (1988). *Knowing children: Participant observation with minors.* Newbury Park, CA: SAGE Publications.

Fortes, M. (1928). *Social and psychological aspects of education in Taleland.* Oxford: Oxford University Press.

Fortes, M. (1949). *The web of kinship among the Tallensi.* Oxford: Oxford University Press.

Freeman, M. & Mathison, S. (2009). *Researching children's experiences.* New York: Guilford Press.

Frønes, I. (1993). Changing childhood. *Childhood* 1 (1): 1–2.

Galman, S. C. (2017). Brave is a dress: Understanding 'good' adults and 'bad' children through adult horror and children's play. *Childhood, 24* (4), 531–544.

Gauntlett, D. (2004). Using creative visual research methods to understand media audiences. *MedienPädagogik,* 4 (1). Retrieved from http://www.medienpaed.com/article/view/60.

Gbadegsin, S. (1998). Individual, community and the moral order. In P. H. Coetzee and A. P. J. Roux (Eds.), *The African philosophy reader,* p. 292–305. London: Routledge.

Gottlieb, A. (2004). *The afterlife is where we come from.* Chicago: University of Chicago Press.

Graue, M. E. & Walsh, D. J. (1998). *Studying children in context: Theories, methods and ethics.* Thousand Oaks, CA: SAGE Publications.

Haas Dyson, A. (2003). *The brothers and sisters learn to write.* New York: Teachers College Press.

Haas Dyson, A. (2001). Donkey Kong in Little Bear country: A first grader's composing development in the media spotlight. *The Elementary School Journal* 101 (4): 417–33.

Hammersley, M. & Atkinson, P. (1995). *Ethnography: Principles in practice.* Abingdon: Routledge.

Harden, J., Scott, S., & Backett-Milburn, K. (2000). Can talk, won't talk. *Sociological Research Online,* 5 (2).

Harkness, S. & Super, C. M. (1986). The developmental niche: A conceptualization at the interface of child and culture. *International Journal of Behavioral Development, 9,* 545-569.

Hill, M. (2006). Children's voices on ways of having a voice: Children and young people's perspectives on methods used in research and consultation. *Childhood, 13,* 69-89.

Hirschfeld, L. A. (2002). Why don't anthropologists like children? *American Anthropologist,* 104 (2), 611–627.

Hymes, D. H. (1974). *Foundations in sociolinguistics: An ethnographic approach.* Philadelphia: University of Pennsylvania Press.

James, A. (1989). Confections, concoctions, and conceptions. *Journal of the Anthropological Society of Oxford,* 10 (2), 83–95.

James, A. (2007). Ethnography in the study of children and childhood. In Atkinson, P., Coffey, A., Delamont, S., Lofland, J. and Lofland, L. (Eds.), *Handbook of Ethnography* (pp. 245–258). London: SAGE Publications.

James, A., Jenks, C. & Prout, A. (1998). *Theorizing childhood.* Cambridge: Polity Press.

Lancy, D. F. (1996). *Playing on the motherground: Cultural routines for children's development.* New York: Guilford Press.

Lareau, A. (2003). *Unequal childhoods: Class, race and family life.* Berkeley, CA: University of California Press.

LeCompte, M. D. & Schensul, J. J. (2016). *The ethnographer's toolkit.* 7 vols. Walnut Creek, CA: Alta Mira Press.

Levine, R. A. (2007). Ethnographic studies of childhood: A historical overview. *American Anthropologist*, 109 (2), 247–260.

Levine, R. A., & New, R. S. (2008). *Anthropology and child development: A cross-cultural reader.* London: Blackwell.

Locke, J. (1996). *Some thoughts concerning education.* Hackett Classics Series. Indianapolis: Hackett Publishing (originally published 1693).

Locke, J. (1998). *An essay concerning human understanding.* Penguin Classics Series. London: Penguin Books (riginally published 1689).

Malinowski, B. (1927). *Sex and repression in savage society.* New York: Harcourt Brace.

Malinowski, B. (1929). *The sexual life of savages: An ethnographic account of courtship, marriage, and family life among the Trobriand Islands, British New Guinea.* New York: Eugenics Publishing Company.

Mandell, N. (1988). The least-adult role in studying children. *Journal of Contemporary Ethnography* 16 (4): 433–467.

Mead, M. (1933). *Coming of age in Samoa.* New York: Blue Ribbon Books.

Mitchell C and Reid-Walsh J (2002). *Researching children's popular culture: The cultural spaces of childhood.* New York: Routledge.

Morton, H. (1996). *Becoming Tongan: An ethnography of childhood.* Honolulu: University of Hawai'i Press.

Nussbaum, M. C. (1997). *Poetic justice: The literary imagination and public life.* Boston: Beacon Press.

Ogbu, J. (1978). *Minority education and caste: The American system in cross-cultural perspective.* New York: Academic Press.

Ogbu, J. (2003). *Black American students in an affluent suburb: a study of academic disengagement.* Mahwah, NJ: Lawrence Erlbaum.

Opie, I. & Opie, P. (1960). *The lore and language of schoolchildren.* Oxford: Clarendon Press.

Opie, I. & Opie, P. (1969). *Children's games.* Oxford: Oxford University Press.

Piaget, J. (1932). *The moral judgement of the child.* New York: Collier.

Pridmore, Pat & G. Lansdown, R. (1997). Exploring children's perceptions of health: Does drawing really break down barriers? *Health Education Journal*, 56. 219–230.

Punch, S. (2002). Research with children: The same or different from research with adults? *Childhood, 9* (3), 321–341.

Rogoff, B. (2003). *The cultural nature of human development.* Oxford: Oxford University Press.

Rossman, G. & Rallis, S. (2017). *An introduction to qualitative method: Learning in the field.* Thousand Oaks, CA: SAGE Publications.

Rousseau, J. J. (1955). *Emile.* London: Everyman's Library (originally published 1672).

Saywitz, K. J. & Camparo, L. B. (2014). *Evidence-based child forensic interviewing: The developmental narrative elaboration interview.* Oxford: Oxford University Press.

Steinberg, S. R. & Kincheloe, J. L. (1997). *Kinderculture: The corporate construction of childhood.* Boulder, CO: Westview Press.

Stokrocki, M., & Samoraj, M. (2002). An ethnographic exploration of children's drawings of their first communion in Poland. *International Journal of Education & the Arts* 3(6).

Super, C. & Harkness, S. (1980). *Anthropological perspectives on child development.* San Francisco: Jossey-Bass.

Super, C. M. (1976). Environmental effects on motor development: The case of African infant precocity. *Developmental Medicine and Child Neurology,* 18, 561–567.

Sutton-Smith, B. (2001). *The ambiguity of play.* Boston: Harvard University Press.

Sutton-Smith, B. (1981). *A history of children's play.* Philadelphia: University of Pennsylvania Press.

Thorne, B. (1993). *Gender play: Girls and boys in school.* New Brunswick, NJ: Rutgers University Press.

Vygotsky, L. S. (1987). Thinking and speech. In R. W. Rieber and A. S. Carton (Eds.), *The collected works of L. S. Vygotsky.* New York: Plenum Books (originally published 1934).

Weber, S. & Mitchell, C. (2000). *That's funny, you don't look like a teacher: Interrogating images and identity in popular culture.* London: Falmer.

Wetton, N. (1999). *Draw and write.* Health Education Unit: University of Southampton.

Whiting, B. B. & Whiting, J. W. (1975). *Children of six cultures.* Cambridge: Harvard University Press.

Winnicott, D. W. (1971). *Therapeutic consultations in child psychiatry.* New York: Basic Books.

Wolcott, H. (1981). Confessions of a trained observer. In T. Popkewitz and B. R. Tabachnik (Eds.), *The study of schooling,* pp. 247–263. New York: Praeger.